The
Bohemian
Flats

The spring flood, from an etching by S. Chatwood Burton

The Bohemian Flats

*Compiled by the Workers of the Writers' Program
of the Work Projects Administration
in the State of Minnesota*

With an Introduction by Thaddeus Radzilowski

MINNESOTA HISTORICAL SOCIETY PRESS
St. Paul • 1986

2004 reprint of 1986 edition

MINNESOTA HISTORICAL SOCIETY PRESS, St. Paul 55101

First published 1941 by the University of Minnesota Press
New material copyright © 1986 by the Minnesota Historical Society

International Standard Book Number 0-87351-200-6
Manufactured in the United States of America
10 9 8 7 6 5 4 3 2 1

Library of Congress Cataloging-in-Publication Data

The Bohemian Flats.

(Borealis books)
Reprint. Originally published: Minneapolis :
University of Minnesota Press, 1941. With new
introd. and index.
Bibliography: p.
1. Czech Americans — Minnesota — Minneapolis — Social
life and customs. 2. Slovak Americans — Minnesota —
Minneapolis — Social life and customs. 3. Bohemian
Flats (Minneapolis, Minn.) — Social life and customs.
4. Minneapolis (Minn.) — Social life and customs.
I. Writers' Program (Minn.)
F614.M56B64   1986   977.6'5790049186   86-12816
ISBN 0-87351-200-6 (pbk.)

Contents

Introduction to the Reprint Edition

Under the impact of industrialization and immigration, American cities often grew like Topsy at the end of the nineteenth century and the beginning of the twentieth. As they grew, they all developed unusual enclaves and neighborhoods marked off from the rest of the city by geography, political boundaries, or industrial development and often distinguished by ethnicity and class. Jones Island off the shores of Milwaukee, with its colony of Kashubian fishermen, and the small mostly Polish city of Hamtramck, nestled in inner-city Detroit, are two of the most prominent examples of these communities. Developers, zoning and planning commissions, and suburban migration have made most of these areas only memories. But because the memories of these enclaves hold the loyalty and imagination of former residents and their fellow citizens, the lost communities are still a significant part of the living tradition that shapes their cities' identities.

Minneapolis's Bohemian Flats is certainly one of these distinctive neighborhoods. Located below the Mississippi River bluffs on which the West Bank Campus of the University of Minnesota is now located, the settlement was razed in the early 1930s to make room for a municipal freight terminal. Despite the more than half a century since the neighborhood's disappearance, it has not been forgotten. Over the years, articles reviewing its history have appeared in the daily press and in local journals.[1] In 1984 the Hennepin County Historical So-

---

[1] See, for example, Lee Clausen, "A New Idea for the Bohemian Flats Mess," *Twin Citian* 10 (Jan. 1968): 12–17; David Wood, "Bohemian Flats Is Long Gone

ciety devoted an issue of its journal, *Hennepin County History*, to the story of Bohemian Flats. The society held several programs that year on the history of the area that drew overflow crowds, attracting hundreds of people interested in this unique aspect of Minneapolis history.[2]

The Bohemian Flats, a history of the area first published in 1941, also helps readers remember the Flats. Only one thousand copies of the book were printed, and it has long been a collector's item for those interested in the history of Minneapolis and its neighborhoods. Beyond the intrinsic fascination of its subject, the book is significant as part of a series of books on the American experience produced by one of the most unusual programs ever established by the United States government: the Federal Writers' Project of the Works Progress Administration (WPA).[3]

The Writers' Project came into being in July 1935 as a national program to give jobs to unemployed writers. The heart of the Writers' Project's work was the guide book series. Each state branch was instructed to create a guide to the state and to its most important cities and interesting locales. Some state projects produced little or nothing of importance; others completed numerous works of enduring value. In all about 400 works were created.

The shapers of the project chose the guide book format for political reasons, fearing to subsidize the imaginative work of writers radicalized by the impact of the Great Depression and

but Memories Linger On," *Minneapolis Tribune*, Aug. 25, 1974; David A. Wood, "How Green Was Their Valley," *Twin Cities* 7 (Dec. 1984): 35–39. St. Paul had similar communities in Swede Hollow and Connemara Patch, both on Phalen Creek, and the Upper Levee, a mostly Italian settlement on the river flats under the High Bridge. See June Drenning Holmquist, ed., *They Chose Minnesota: A Survey of the State's Ethnic Groups* (St. Paul: Minnesota Historical Society Press, 1981), 138, 262, 453.

[2] Dave Wood, "Bohemian Flats," *Minneapolis Tribune*, Apr. 14, 1984, p. 1C.

[3] In 1939 the Works Progress Administration was renamed the Works Projects Administration, and the Writers' Project became the Writers' Program. For a summary of the beginnings of the WPA Writers' Project, here and below, see Jerre Mangione, *The Dream and the Deal: The Federal Writers' Project, 1935–1943* (Boston: Little, Brown, and Co., 1972; Philadelphia: University of Pennsylvania Press, 1983), 29–50, 329–30.

[viii

their own poverty. Painters and sculptors would not cause too much trouble, the officials reasoned, so they could be allowed to work on projects of their own choosing, but writers' works might prove embarrassing or troublesome to the agency that was paying their salaries. The guide book series was a way of creating employment without creating controversy.

Those hired by the Writers' Project ranged from the barely literate to writers of great talent. The major requirement for employment was to be on relief, and several writers had to find ways of getting on the welfare rolls before they could be hired. Writers of the caliber of Saul Bellow and Richard Wright worked on the project; Meridel Le Sueur is Minnesota's most distinguished alumna. A surprising number of misfits and crackpots also participated. In urban areas such as Chicago or New York, the Writers' Project could draw on a rich pool of talented and experienced writers. In other areas it was not so easy to put together a staff. Dr. Mabel Ulrich, a physician who headed the Minnesota project, explained the difficulty:

> I signed my name and Mr. G [the WPA administrator setting up the program] got right down to business. Could I collect two hundred and fifty writers from the State in ten days? Our State is the largest in the Middle West and is about fifty per cent agricultural. Was it possible, I wondered, that we could have that many mute inglorious authors? It didn't seem likely. But he was confident and, for all I knew, there might be hundreds hiding their frustrations on our farms and lurking unrecognized in our few cities. . . .
>
> The next morning I went to the relief office to hunt through the files for the writers I was to interview. But they were either too modest or too fearful to classify themselves as such. A small handful confessed to having worked on newspapers, but that was all. In the end I added to these the cards of college and normal school graduates, teachers, and writers of advertising. Day after day now I interviewed these men and women. . . .
>
> All who claimed newspaper experience I accepted at once, but it began to look as if such bona fide writers as

the State possessed were either subsidized by relatives or making an adequate living. Before the interviewing was over our quota had been reduced a hundred from that first suggested, and it was tacitly conceded for emergency purposes the designation *writer* might be interpreted with considerable latitude. I chose one hundred and twenty from the neediest and most promising, and praying that release from economic pressure would release talent as well, I assigned them to work.[4]

The guide books, intended to tell the reader about every aspect of the geography, history, and culture of a state or city, often focused on ethnic groups and distinct neighborhoods, but the coverage, of necessity, was usually brief, superficial, and often clichéd. Washington's advice to the Minnesota project to get more information on ethnic groups reflected this attitude. "Your essay on racial customs lacks color," the Minnesotans were told. "Surely there must be folk-dancing and Old World costumes to be observed."[5]

It was not until late in the project that a serious effort was made to document the ethnic and cultural diversity of the United States. The national director of the Writers' Project, Henry Alsberg, concerned that the guide books would not give a comprehensive picture of the United States, began to encourage state offices to undertake individual studies that focused on the many ethnic groups in America. A number of states had published studies of ethnic groups by 1938, but these were based largely on secondary sources and hence offered little new information. In addition, the writing was poor and some were not even published in English.[6]

In 1938, in order to develop a new series of books on ethnic groups based on primary research and written to a high literary standard, Alsberg hired Morton W. Royce as a national

---

[4] Mabel S. Ulrich, "Salvaging Culture for the WPA," *Harper's Magazine* 178 (May 1939): 654-55.

[5] Ulrich, "Salvaging Culture," 656.

[6] For an account of the ethnic studies project, see Mangione, *The Dream and the Deal*, 277-85.

consultant for social-ethnic studies. Royce, who held two doctorates from Columbia, had written an influential study of European minority groups. In his first letter to the state directors announcing the new program, he displayed the broad sense of cultural pluralism that was to be the hallmark of his program. He wrote: "The building up of our country knows no parallel in historical times — in the influx of peoples from all ends of the earth, and in the freedom and opportunity which beckoned to the impoverished and oppressed of all lands. How a social and cultural unity was achieved by these people, without stamping cultural differences into one mold, producing the unique American civilization, and how this fabric of American democracy was progressively enlarged, is the crux of our story."[7] A month after Royce was hired, Benjamin Botkin, a leading folklorist, joined the project, and the two agreed to work in close collaboration and to include the collection of folklore as part of the ethnic studies project.

Although Royce threw himself into the work — in the words of one contemporary, "with demonic vitality" — the results were disappointing. Personality conflicts and turf battles with state directors and directors of other special projects such as the southern oral-life history project, as well as the loss of the support of Alsberg, who resigned in 1939, undermined Royce's ability to move his plans along. At the same time the Writers' Project itself was beginning to unravel. Congress cut back funding drastically in 1939, necessitating wholesale layoffs and the termination of many worthwhile projects, including some of those initiated by Royce and Botkin. In addition, national support for the Writers' Project was being eroded by the witch hunt initiated by Congressman Martin Dies and his newly formed Committee to Investigate Un-American Activities. The Project was tarred by Dies as a haven for Reds and its works were denounced as contaminated with Communist propaganda.[8] In 1940, Royce left the Writers' Project, and the eth-

[7] Quoted in Mangione, *The Dream and the Deal*, 278.
[8] Mangione, *The Dream and the Deal*, 4–20.

nic studies series petered out far short of its projected goal of 160 volumes, having produced only a few works.

One of the books, however, that came out of the ethnic studies effort was *The Bohemian Flats*. Ironically, we know more about the people of the Bohemian Flats than we do about the people who researched and wrote it. Perhaps Lee Grove, Gladys Fleischauer, and Irving Cohen were part of that cadre of enthusiastic amateurs recruited from the relief rolls by Mabel Ulrich and perhaps it was on this project that those needy and promising would-be-writers saw, as Ulrich prayed, their talents released. The book was sponsored by the Hennepin County Historical Society and published for the Writers' Program — it was renamed in 1939 — by the University of Minnesota Press. Jerre Mangione, in his history of the Writers' Project, writes that the work "contained some fascinating material about a settlement of Bohemian, Irish, Lithuanian and Danish immigrants which the city of Minneapolis wiped out . . . to make room for wharves and railroad yards; although better written than most of the Project's ethnic studies, it suffered from undue brevity."[9]

Bohemian Flats was more than a solid and unpatronizing study of an ethnic neighborhood in Minneapolis. It and the ethnic studies project of the WPA were monuments to a change that had taken place in the popular consciousness of America. It is unlikely that such a sympathetic study would have been written and published only a decade and a half earlier.

Nativism flourished in the United States at the beginning of the century, and it was notoriously strong in Minneapolis; this nativism turned into the virulent antiforeign and antiradical hysteria of World War I and its aftermath. "One hundred percent Americanism" was the watchword, and the violation of the civil rights of aliens and foreign-born citizens became the order of the day. By 1924 laws restricting immigration — motivated in part by racism, bigotry, and fear — kept out all but a minuscule handful of Eastern and Southern European immigrants. The country found itself gripped by another wave

---

[9] Mangione, *The Dream and the Deal*, 284–85.

of nativism in 1928 with the Democratic party's nomination of Al Smith for president. This time it was the Catholicism of the Irish, Germans, and Southern and Eastern Europeans that marked them as dangerous to the American polity and unfit to take their places as citizens equal to the Protestant descendants of earlier immigrants.[10]

Despite its fearful power, American nativism lost force with surprising rapidity in the 1930s. A more tolerant and benign view of the immigrants and their children began to take shape in the public consciousness. Although Americans were still committed to assimilation, they seemed willing to give cultural pluralism a trial. The decline in the number of aliens aided the transition, as did the appearance of writers and artists from the new immigrant groups (such as Jerre Mangione and Louis Adamic) who won audiences for a more sympathetic view of the newcomers and their children; the tendency was given legitimacy by Franklin D. Roosevelt's New Deal.[11]

New Dealers were much more sympathetic to the immigrants than their Republican predecessors. Although none of the laws governing immigration or aliens was repealed, they were now enforced with sympathy, not the hostility of the 1920s. Roosevelt himself accepted the existence of ethnic groups as a feature of national life. In 1935 he allotted funds to the Office of Education for publications and broadcasts that would "reveal the rich heritages that have come to us through the many races and nationalities which make up our population."[12] The best known of the programs was a twenty-six-part radio series broadcast in 1938–39 entitled "Americans All . . . Immigrants All." It is clear that the WPA ethnic project,

[10] On nativism, see John Higham, *Strangers in the Land: Patterns of American Nativism, 1860–1925* (New Brunswick, N.J.: Rutgers University Press, 1955; New York: Atheneum, 1973), and Robert K. Murray, *Red Scare: A Study in National Hysteria, 1919–1920* (Minneapolis: University of Minnesota Press, 1955).

[11] In 1930 aliens made up only 4.7 percent of the U.S. population; by 1940 the percentage was down to 1.3. *Historical Statistics of the United States: Colonial Times to 1957* (Washington, D.C.: Government Printing Office, 1960), 65.

[12] Quoted in Richard Weiss, "Ethnicity and Reform: Minorities and the Ambience of the Depression Years," *Journal of American History* 66 (Dec. 1979): 568.

conceived at the same time, reflected this new initiative of Roosevelt's government.[13]

Tolerance for racial and ethnic differences also developed in reaction to the racial theories of the Nazis. Those relegated to subhuman status, Jews and Slavs, were the very peoples who had been the targets of American nativism. As one historian of the period has observed, "Tendencies toward greater ethnic democracy in the United States were strengthened by the need to contrast American freedom to Nazi tyranny. The identification of totalitarianism with the ruthless repression of ethnic minorities resulted in the counteridentification of democracy with minority group encouragement and tolerance."[14] These popular developments coincided with the full-scale academic attack on racial theories by anthropologist Franz Boas and his students at Columbia University. By the end of the 1930s, most of these racial dogmas lost every shred of scholarly legitimacy. Thus the prevailing intellectual and political climate not only made possible new popular studies of ethnicity such as *The Bohemian Flats* but also assured them of a ready and sympathetic audience.

The tone that pervades *The Bohemian Flats* reflects these attitudes toward ethnicity. It depicts a happy, peaceful society united by generous neighborliness and enthusiastic, unselfconscious participation in colorful rites and customs. The world on the riverbank seems to have no serious frictions or manifestations of antisocial behavior. It is a genuine community. While the descriptions are still touched by the sense of the exotic that marked most writing about immigrant neighborhoods, it is more friendly than earlier accounts. More importantly, the Flats are invested with the kind of meaning that had usually been reserved only for the farming village or the small town. The book enshrines the immigrant neighborhood as a species of the vanishing American community doomed by the march of progress and industry. One reviewer, who accurately caught the book's nostalgia for lost community, wrote

[13] Weiss, "Ethnicity and Reform," 568–69.
[14] Weiss, "Ethnicity and Reform," 566.

that it "reminds us that the development of industry and commerce is sometimes possible only by sacrificing the picturesque nonconformity of our ancestors."[15] It is clear that by 1941 the immigrants of Bohemian Flats were on their way into the pantheon that houses the Pilgrims, the pioneers, and other mythic ancestors.

The same reviewer also warned that "one suspects that life on the levee was less idyllic than the writers of this book would have one believe."[16] Some other critics were less circumspect. Almost immediately after the publication of *The Bohemian Flats*, Bessie Douglas of Minneapolis wrote to Robert Scott, president of the Hennepin County Historical Society, to record another view of the area. As a young Presbyterian Sunday-school teacher sent to work on the Flats in the late 1880s, she was warned that she should never visit the homes of her students without a man along. She remembered that "it was not safe and even at that time Police protection was sometimes necessary for the men if they went down at night. There were drunken fights on the Flats and sometimes stories of knifings." Some of the students she taught came from "dreadful homes." One of them, for example, was from a family in which the mother had died, the father was an abusive alcoholic, and the sister was a prostitute.[17] The 1937 official history of the Westminister Presbyterian Church, for which Douglas worked, noted that "Police were needed for a time even in the daylight

[15] John T. Flanagan, Review of *The Bohemian Flats, Minnesota History* 23 (Mar. 1942): 69. For another review, see *Minneapolis Sunday Tribune and Star-Journal*, Jan. 4, 1942, sec.1, p. 12.

[16] Flanagan, Review, 69. The rowdy beer parties described on p. 22–23 are the only exception, and they are attributed to the immigrants going "wild over their freedom" in America after being repressed in Europe. There is no hint that they may have been seeking relief from the dangerous drudgery of life at the bottom of American industrial society.

[17] Mrs. George P. Douglas to Robert E. Scott, Jan. 8, 1942, in Bohemian Flats File, Hennepin County Historical Society, Minneapolis. One long-time resident of the Flats recalled, "They had some wild fights over there [under the bridge]. I remember once eight paddy wagons came down. But I stayed away from there. They were liable to have stickers or lead-shooters." *Minneapolis Star*, May 18, 1963, p. 5A.

to protect the [church] workers in what was called one of the worst holes in the city, 'Hell's Kitchen.' "[18]

Even taking into account the pious horror and the exaggerated anxieties of comfortable, middle-class Anglo-Saxons working in a raw immigrant shanty town, it does appear that, at least early in its history, the Bohemian Flats was "not a friendly zone," in the words of the church historian. These characterizations, however, described the period when the influx of new immigrants, mainly young males, was at its height. By the turn of the century, life had settled somewhat as the immigrants began to raise families, and the rate of immigration to the neighborhood slowed. As a result even the church workers remarked on the growing peacefulness of the area, which they, of course, attributed to their own work.[19] The post–World War I community, which was probably best remembered by the project's informants, was made up largely of middle-aged householders of long tenure in the neighborhood. If not idyllic, it was at least probably a quite peaceful and less densely populated place in which neighbors of many years had come to terms with each other's foibles and eccentricities and had shared most of life's passages.[20]

The Bohemian Flats tells us little about the less attractive aspects of life on the river, and it is also silent about the larger Flats settlement. The book describes only the area known as the Washington Avenue Addition, that is, the area bounded by the Washington Avenue bridge and South 2nd Street on the south and the plant of the Minneapolis Brewing and Malting

[18] John Edward Bushnell, *The History of Westminister Presbyterian Church of Minneapolis, Minnesota, 1907–37* (Minneapolis: The Church, 1937), 85. Douglas's letter quoted this passage and those reproduced below.

[19] Bushnell, in his History (p. 86), proclaims proudly: "It would be difficult to find any church elsewhere that has had equal success in transforming character and rebuilding a whole community."

[20] A map prepared in 1984 by John Stanko, a former Flats resident, showed the location of the homes of over sixty of the families living in the Flats in 1922; it is reproduced in Deacon John Matlov, "Slovak Flats: Gone But Not Forgotten," in *Furdek 1985* (Cleveland: First Catholic Ladies Slovak Assn., 1985), 135. Many of the same families appear in the 1900 census (see note 21), often at the same location.

Association on the north, and encompassing the entire length of Wood Street and the two blocks each of Mill and Cooper streets with street addresses of fifty and higher. Most later writers on the subject have referred to the same area. Yet the Washington Avenue Addition was only a part of a larger settlement on the Flats along the river that extended north to the beginnings of Mill and Cooper streets and south for several blocks beyond the bridge. The area south of the bridge included 22nd Avenue South between Washington Avenue South and South 3rd Street and 22½ Avenue South between South 2½ Street and South 3rd Street. It was this entire area — now the white space on the city map east of the angle formed by South 4th Street and 21st Avenue South — that the newspapers of the day called "Bohemian Flats."

There are good reasons, as we shall see, for distinguishing the Washington Avenue Addition, but it is important to note also how it fit into the whole settlement on the riverbank. In terms of lot size and density of settlement, the Washington Avenue Addition was of a piece with the extensions of Mill and Cooper streets to the north of it. The homes were smaller and more tightly packed together on smaller lots than those to the south of the Washington Avenue bridge, where lots were two or three times larger with fewer and more spacious homes on them. Generally the immigrants who had come earlier and held better-paying jobs lived south of the bridge. It is interesting to note that a number of the important informants to the project, such as Thomas Shafar and his wife Rose, had lived in the South Flats since before the turn of the century. This may help to account for the benign picture of life on the Flats that the book gives us.

The distinctions between the areas north and south of the bridge were not only social and economic but were also ethnic. The 1900 United States census, taken at about the midpoint of the history of the community, gives us a good overview of the immigrants' ethnicities. In the area to the north of the bridge, which includes the Washington Avenue Addition, there were 613 Slovaks, 123 Swedes, 90 Czechs or Bohemians, 41 Irish, 27 Norwegians, 10 Poles, 5 Germans, 4 Austrians, 2 Danes, 1

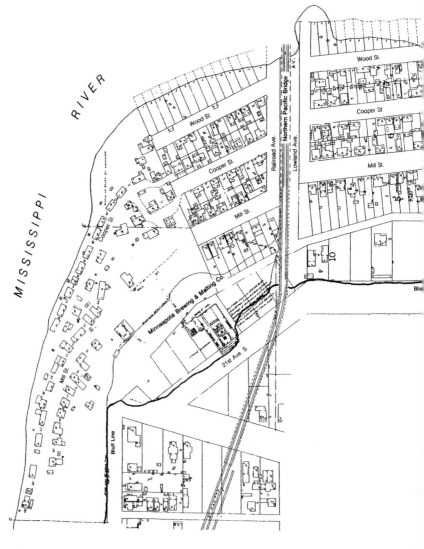

[xviii

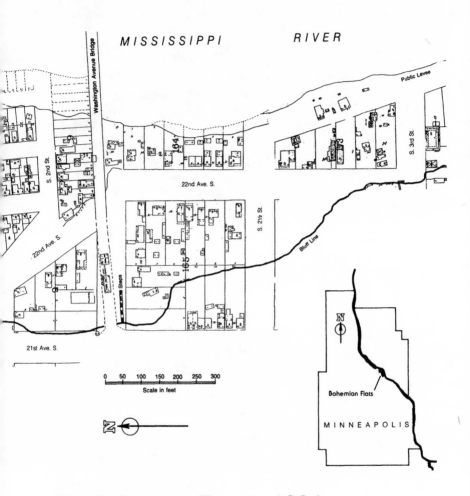

The Bohemian Flats in 1904

Russian, and a dozen children of mixed marriages between Germans and Swedes, Slovaks and Czechs, and Austrians and Slovaks. Three-fourths of the Czechs lived on the upper levee in the high-rent areas of Mill Street and the small spur of 22nd Avenue South that is north of the bridge or on the larger lots on South 2nd Street at the southern end of the Washington Avenue Addition. A similar percentage of the Swedes were clustered at the extreme northern end of Mill and Cooper streets outside of Bohemian Flats proper, and a few others were found on South 2nd Street. Thus the Washington Avenue Addition, especially the lower level near the river, was overwhelmingly a Slovak settlement. If anything, "Bohemian Flats" should have been known as "Slovak Flats."[21]

"Bohemian Flats" should have been the designation of the area south of the Washington Avenue bridge. In that section there were 105 Czechs, 85 Swedes, 23 Germans, 22 Slovaks, 16 Norwegians, 8 Irish, 7 Swiss, 2 Finns, 2 native-born Americans of native parents, 1 Dane, and 13 children of mixed Swedish-Norwegian or Swedish-Finnish ancestry. Almost all the Czechs lived on 22 or 22½ Avenues South. Of the six Slovak families in the area two each lived on 22 and 22½ Avenues South and one each near the water's edge on Washington Avenue and South 3rd Street. Half the Swedes and almost all the Norwegians lived on South 3rd Street at the extreme southern end of the district. The ten German households were evenly scattered throughout the area, with at least one on each street.[22]

[21] This and subsequent demographic data is taken from manuscript census schedules, U.S. Bureau of the Census, Twelfth Census of the United States, 1900, Hennepin County, Minnesota, Ward 5, Enumeration District 67, Sheets 1–18. For information on the history of these groups in Minnesota, see Holmquist, ed., *They Chose Minnesota*. In referring to various ethnic groups, I am lumping together immigrants and their children, including those born in the U.S.

[22] In addition to providing a general picture of the residents of the river flats, the census data hint at a variety of fascinating individual stories, such as that of the only Jewish resident of the area, a Russian immigrant day laborer who boarded with a Slovak family, or the couple (both of whom had Irish-born parents) with the husband born in New York and the wife in Hindustan. In light of the later eviction of the residents, it is interesting to note that 95 percent of the residents reported themselves as home owners.

Table 1. Dates of Immigration for Largest Groups on Bohemian Flats

	Before 1880	1880–84	1885–89	1890–94	1895–99
Slovaks	6%	36%	25%	13%	20%
Czechs	25%	42%	33%		
Irish	30%	70%			
Swedes	34%	22%	22%	22%	

The immigration dates of the groups show that the Slovaks constituted almost all of the recent immigrants on the Flats. Only the Poles, Swedes, and Slovaks showed any newcomers after 1890, and only the Slovaks had immigrants who arrived after 1895 (see Table 1). Almost sixty Slovaks were lodgers in the homes of fellow immigrants, a pattern more common to recent arrivals. All of the other groups except the Poles showed fewer than five lodgers. (Half the Poles in the Flats boarded with one of the two Polish families.)

The vast majority of all the immigrants living north of the bridge listed their occupation simply as "day laborer," with only a handful listing other occupations such as policeman, stationary engineer, bartender, painter, iron worker, and flour mill worker. It is clear, however, that many of the day laborers, especially those who headed households or had been in the United States for some time, had arranged steady work with one or more employers, because they reported continuous employment. On the other hand, younger men and recent arrivals, often lodgers, reported in many cases one or more months of unemployment during 1899.

While there were a number of day laborers among those south of the bridge, the majority reported more substantial occupations. For example, on one side of South 22nd Street there lived a cornice maker, a cabinet maker, a policeman, a cooper, a stonemason, a bricklayer, two brewery workers, two mill workers, a salesman, three day laborers and a janitor. Half the families also had two or more adults who were employed.

Most of the second generation, especially those living north of the bridge, were too young to work and were listed as either at school or at home. Two hundred and thirty-five of the Slovaks and sixty Swedes, for example, were children either at school or at home because they were too young for school. Most members of the second generation who reported employment had better-paying or more skilled occupations than their fathers, although four Swedes and twelve Slovaks of that generation were day laborers. Sons of some skilled workers, especially coopers, followed their fathers' occupations. Fewer than ten immigrant women worked outside the home. (There were only four households headed by women.) Those who did listed one of four occupations: laundress, domestic, seamstress, or day laborer. More than two dozen women cared for boarders in addition to their own families. Their daughters worked as saleswomen, dressmakers, cashiers, seamstresses, packers in mills or crockery factories, or workers in woolen mills.

Ole E. Rølvaag, in his novel *The Boat of Longing*, gave voice to a view still widely held in the 1910s of the Bohemian Flats and its people as a world and society apart, alien and detached from the city within which they found themselves. He wrote: "Obviously there were oceans and whole continents lying between this place and the one above, even though only a bridge separated them."[23]

Was the gulf between the Flats and the rest of the city as wide as Rølvaag so dramatically pictured it? The answer varied for individual residents, of course, by ethnicity, gender, and age. Most of the men went into the city to work (or at least to seek work) six days a week, and they spent most of the daytime hours in the society of outsiders. Most of the children of the immigrants over seven years of age also left the Flats each day for school or to go to apprenticeships or work places. Most of the women, on the other hand, remained on the Flats in the company of each other and the young children. Few of them had opportunities to learn much about the city that loomed over them or even to master English. The census taker reported that not many of the more recent immigrants among

[23] Rølvaag, *The Boat of Longing* (New York: Harper Brothers, 1922; St. Paul: Minnesota Historical Society Press, Borealis Books, 1985), 108.

the women (who often came later than their husbands anyway) had any knowledge of English.

Some of the ethnic groups on the Flats were probably tied into the society of the district above them, which was overwhelmingly Swedish, Norwegian, and German. As on the Flats, the Swedes were the largest of the Northern and Western European groups settled on the heights next to the river. Thus the Czechs and Slovaks in the Flats community were the only representatives of their groups in the entire surrounding district. The small number of mixed marriages recorded by 1900 between Czechs and Slovaks, some of whom had been living together for two decades, indicates that the two groups probably socialized little with each other, as well.[24]

The Slavic and Irish inhabitants of the riverbank were also probably separated from their Scandinavian, Anglo-Saxon, and German neighbors on the Flats and above by their political preferences. The Congressional district in which the Flats was located regularly voted almost two to one for the Republicans, with some wards going as high as five to one. The ward that included the Flats and the area above, however, usually split close to fifty-fifty between the parties, with an occasional Democratic party candidate winning a majority in the area. Since there is no reason to believe that the voting preferences of Scandinavians in the ward varied from other Scandinavians in the district, it is likely that the Democratic votes came largely from Eastern Europeans and Irish Catholics on the Flats.[25]

Nothing separated the people on the Flats from each other and tied them to communities elsewhere in the city more than

[24] In the entire Flats settlement, there were only about a dozen mixed marriages, including four Slovak-Czech unions. There was one Czech-Irish marriage between two American-born children of immigrants recorded in 1900 — a harbinger of greater interaction among the children of the immigrants, who shared a common history on the Flats and common experience at school or work.

[25] See, for example, Election Results, Hennepin County, 1902 SAM66, Roll 12, and 1904 SAM66, Roll 14, Minnesota Historical Society. The Democratic party's candidates for auditor and city attorney, for example, carried the Flats area in 1904, and the other Democratic candidates were within two to fifteen votes of winning the area, while losing badly elsewhere in the district.

religious affiliation. (Despite their extensive acknowledgements to numerous clergymen for assistance in tracing church history, the writers of *The Bohemian Flats* devoted only two pages to this significant aspect of the area's history.) The Scandinavians who lived primarily on the edges of the riverbank settlement by the end of the century worshiped in churches at the top of the bluff. They had been displaced quickly and early from the center of the Flats. In 1888, less than two decades after the first settlement in the Flats, the Swedes sold their church on Cooper Street to Andrew Kocisko, who bought it for what became the first Slovak Lutheran congregation, Holy Emmanuel.[26] The Swedes and Norwegians from the Flats were swallowed up into the congregations above the Flats and no single church they attended was identified with the riverbank people.

The religous situation among the Slavs was more complicated. The Czechs were divided between Catholics and Free Thinkers, with the former group being the larger. The Slovaks were initially separated into three main groups: Lutherans, who numbered more than three-fifths of the Slovak population; Roman Catholics, who made up about a third of the group; and a small number of Greek Catholics. The proportions reflected the vagaries of chance that governed the selection of settlement sites by immigrants. In Slovakia, almost three-quarters of the population was Roman Catholic, while Lutherans made up only about 12 percent.[27]

At first, Greek Catholic and Roman Catholic Slovaks and some of the Roman Catholic Czechs worshiped together at the Polish Church of the Holy Cross in Northeast Minneapolis.

[26] Interview by W. Lestrude of Andrew Kocisko, Nov. 11, 1938, in Hennepin County Historical Society.

[27] The material on Slovak and Czech congregations is drawn from Mark Stolarik, "The Slovaks," in Holmquist, ed., *They Chose Minnesota*, 355, and Rev. Stanley Srnec, "A History of Our Lady of Perpetual Help Parish," typescript, [1957–1963], in Bohemian Flats File, Hennepin County Historical Society. I am also indebted to Professor Keith P. Dyrud of Augsburg College and Mr. John Kovach of Minneapolis, a member of Immanuel Baptist Church, for sharing their knowledge of local church history with me.

Some of the other Czechs attended services at the German Church of St. Elizabeth at South 8th Street and 15th Avenue South, which was closer to the Flats. Czechs and Slovaks combined to create the Sts. Cyril and Methodius Society, a fraternal insurance group, which later became a charter lodge of the First Catholic Slovak Union. In 1891, with a Moravian priest available, members of the society received permission to found their own church, St. Cyril's, to serve the Flats and Northeast settlements. Shortly afterward, a group of Flats dwellers, apparently primarily Czechs, withdrew their support. They continued to worship at St. Elizabeth's until the priest from St. Cyril's was persuaded to move back from Northeast Minneapolis to found a new parish, Our Lady of Perpetual Help, on South 21st Street. This became the primary Czech church, while most of the Slovak Catholics continued to travel each Sunday to St. Cyril's in Northeast Minneapolis. A former pastor of Our Lady of Perpetual Help noted wryly that Slovaks from the Flats were welcomed only grudgingly until the congregation decided to build a new church in the 1920s and needed more contributors. Internal difficulties at St. Cyril's may also have encouraged the change of allegiance by some Slovaks to Our Lady of Perpetual Help.

The Greek Catholics continued to worship at either the Polish church or the new St. Cyril's until they joined with their Rusin and Ukrainian co-religionists to found St. John's Byzantine Rite Church in Northeast Minneapolis in 1907. The Ukrainians withdrew in 1913 to establish their own church leaving St. John's to the Slovaks and Rusins. Thus the Greek Catholic Slovaks, like their Catholic brethren, traveled more than forty blocks each Sunday to go to church. By the time the Flats were cleared in the 1930s, the Greek Catholic Slovaks had merged almost completely into the larger Rusin community. Today there is little memory in the church of the Slovak origin of some of the founders. A few of the Greek Catholic Slovaks may also have been involved in the founding of St. Mary's Greek Catholic Church in Northeast Minneapolis in 1887 and may have seceded to the Russian Orthodox Church with the congregation after its celebrated dispute with Roman Catholic Archbishop John Ireland.[28]

The Slovak Evangelical Church of Holy Emmanuel (originally St. Emmanuel), as *The Bohemian Flats* reminds us (p. 26–27), was the church most identified with the Flats community. Founded with the assistance of a German pastor, it became part of the Missouri Synod. The church remained in the Flats until the beginning of the twentieth century, when it moved up to the top of the bluff. Crowded out by the expansion of the University of Minnesota, the congregation finally settled in 1970 in the Minneapolis suburb of Bloomington. For more than thirty years Holy Emmanuel served more members of the Flats community than any other church.

In the early 1920s a group of dissident members who favored greater lay control and a less conservative theology withdrew to found Holy Trinity Lutheran on 29th Avenue South in South Minneapolis. By the end of the 1930s the congregation had grown larger than Holy Emmanuel. In 1956, the congregation built a new church, Prince of Glory Lutheran, in a newer area of South Minneapolis; it was affiliated with the Lutheran Church in America.

In addition to the Lutheran secession, Holy Emmanuel also suffered a loss to the Baptists. Shortly before World War I, a young Moravian Baptist woman, Mary Vrastir, who had earlier emigrated to Canada, arrived in Minneapolis to attend Northwest Baptist Seminary conducted by the well-known Baptist minister W. B. Riley. Assigned to assist a seminary mission in the Seven Corners area, Vrastir turned her attention to the nearby Slovak settlement and soon made a number of converts among some of the women from the village of Važec in the Liptov region of Slovakia. By 1917, the converts were numerous enough to establish their first church in a garage on Washington Avenue. Eventually, with their congregation grown to thirty-three families, the Slovak Baptists were able to acquire a regular church. The Baptists apparently won all of

[28] On the dispute, see Keith P. Dyrud, "East Slavs," in Holmquist, ed., *They Chose Minnesota*, 408.

their converts from among the Lutherans. In 1986 the Slovak Baptist church, Immanuel Baptist, was on 36th Avenue in South Minneapolis.

While other groups, such as Seventh-Day Adventists, also made inroads in the Flats settlements, one of the most extensive efforts came from Westminister Presbyterian Church. Taking over a mission church founded by Plymouth Presbyterian, Westminister began a broad program of Sunday school instruction, sewing and cooking classes, a free library, day nursery, kindergarten, and dispensary. The church gave out food and clothing to the needy and ran excursions to the country for children who lived on the Flats. The mission building was twice enlarged before a new one was built on South 2½ Street. In 1913 the congregation constructed a new chapel at 20th Avenue South and Riverside Avenue, which remained the center for its missionary work, later becoming an independent church and, in 1970, the Cedar-Riverside People's Community Center. Although the church evidently won some adherents among the residents of the Flats, its proselytizing effort was not as successful as that of the Baptists. No independent Presbyterian congregation was established, and the chapel remained a dependent outpost of the mother church. The philanthropy practiced by church workers probably constituted the main contribution of the Presbyterians to the Flats settlement and provided many Flats residents with their only sustained contact with middle-class, Anglo-Saxon, American life and values.[29]

When this book first appeared, however, middle-class, Anglo-Saxon America was again changing its perceptions of the immigrants. Ironically, the expansion of cultural pluralism that characterized the 1930s was cut short when the United States actually went to war against Fascism in December 1941, the same month the book was published. Only for Japanese immigrants and their children did the level of violence and hostility reach that marked in World War I. Nevertheless,

[29] On the activities of Presbyterians on the Flats, see Douglas to Scott, Jan. 8, 1942.

fears of disloyalty and suspicion of those who seemed to be foreign reappeared. Conformity and Americanization were the goals of wartime America. In the name of unity the melting pot was turned into a pressure cooker; differences lost their charm and the new government-sponsored ethnic studies now searched for the potential dangers that lurked in the maintenance of ethnicity.[30] Some government officials even suggested massive government programs of Americanization to reduce friction and "save" the ethnics from the expected hostility of the natives.[31] By 1942, the possibility of new ethnic studies was again becoming remote.

Life on the Flats continued for several years after *The Bohemian Flats* was published. But one by one, the fourteen remaining houses were abandoned or moved. The last home on the Upper Flats was destroyed in 1963 to make way for the new Washington Avenue bridge.[32]

The settlement on the river flats was a curious one. Marked off from the majority culture of the surrounding city by ethnicity, language, religion, class, and geography, the residents found themselves separated from each other by all of the same factors except geography. While the neighborhood gave them one strong identity, the institutions around which most immigrant settlements organized themselves — their churches — gave them a multiplicity of others that tied many of them to other neighborhoods and distant people. Those factors make

[30] See, for example, "Social Dynamics in Detroit," Dec. 3, 1942, Office of War Information Surveys, Record Group 44, Box 1814, National Archives.

[31] Alan Cranston, a young bureaucrat in the Office of Facts and Figures who would later become a U.S. senator from California, suggested one such plan in a memo titled "A Program for American Unity." He concludes: "A mounting discrimination is slowly dividing Americans, segregating them, turning them against one another and against America. This smoldering suspicion against all peoples of recent foreign backgrounds is an increasingly serious threat to American unity and the success of the war effort." Memorandum to Mr. Allen Grover from Alan Cranston, Jan. 13, 1942, Office of War Information, Office of Facts and Figures 1941–42: Racial and Alien Questions, Record Group 208, Box 66, National Archives.

[32] *Minneapolis Star*, May 18, 1963, p. 5A.

the Flats a unique immigrant district. We are fortunate that *The Bohemian Flats* was one of the few studies in the WPA ethnic series that was completed, so that the story of this unusual and charming chapter in the history of Minneapolis and the history of immigration was not lost.

THADDEUS RADZILOWSKI

Foreword

There are many persons living in and around the Twin Cities whose relatives lived on the Flats. Many of them, prominent in the cities' civic and cultural life, experienced meager beginnings there; others knew the Flats only from the Mississippi River bridge. From the vantage point of the high cliff on the university side of the river, generations of students, too, stealing a few minutes' rest or holding a tryst on a sunny knoll, have looked across to observe the activities of the Flats. In the old days the idling student always saw something to hold his attention—chickens, ducks, dogs, and goats, once in a while a stray cow, a yard full of driftwood or lines of washing, innumerable children. He looked down upon a peaceful, quiet world, far afield from the university rush and the bustle of city life just over the hill.

The Flats settlement in Minneapolis is unique. In other communities throughout the country there have been similar sections settled by foreign groups who came to make their homes in America. Other cities have had their own little Europes along the river or across the tracks or in the hollow. But this Bohemian Flats, always physically separated from the metropolis growing around it, has had a peculiarly arresting history and a persistent appeal.

It is the duty of the historical societies to have such stories written and preserved for posterity. In a real sense they are wonderful stories. They are the records of citizens and local history in the making, of common folk whose influence has been felt over an entire locality.

ROBERT E. SCOTT, *President*
Hennepin County Historical Society

Acknowledgments

We have endeavored to make the story of the Bohemian Flats as simple and forthright as the lives of the people it portrays. Insofar as we have been successful in this, thanks are due in large part to three former members of our staff, Lee Grove and Gladys Fleischauer, who laid the groundwork, and Irving Cohen, who wrote the final narrative.

There are of course many others who have shared prominently in the work. On special technical problems we are grateful for the advice of Esther Jerabek of the Minnesota Historical Society library staff; the Reverend George S. Dargay of St. Cyril's Catholic Church; E. R. T. Peterson of the Minneapolis City Engineer's Office; Richard Wiggin, Minneapolis city attorney; and the departments of geology and botany of the University of Minnesota.

In tracing church history, we have had the advice of former pastors of St. Emmanuel's Slovak Lutheran Church, the Reverend Karl Hauser and the Reverend J. M. Vrudny, and of the present pastor, the Reverend Ernest Reguly; of the Reverend V. Vojta, pastor of the First Slovak Baptist Church; and of the pastor of Our Lady of Perpetual Help Catholic Church, the Reverend J. F. Hovorka.

In permitting us to use one of his unpublished etchings of the Bohemian Flats, Professor S. Chatwood Burton of the University of Minnesota has made a priceless contribution to the book. Invaluable assistance was given by Joseph Zalusky, who put his personal collection of photographs at our disposal and permitted us to reproduce two of them. The Twin City public libraries, the Minnesota Historical Society, the Minneapolis *Times,* and the Minneapolis *Star Journal* also cooperated generously in making their picture files available to us. Four views of the present-day Flats were supplied by the Minnesota WPA Information Service; and George E. Luxton granted us permission to use his rare photograph of the Flats in 1910. Line drawings are the work of Margaret Martin of the Minnesota WPA Art Project.

We are indebted to Paul Radosavljevich of New York City for permission to quote from the translation of "Where Is My Home?" as it originally appeared in his book, *Who Are the Slavs?*

With particular gratitude we acknowledge our debt to the many individuals, most of whom have lived or still live on the Flats, who told us their stories. Without the friendly assistance and endless patience of these collaborators, the book could not have been written: Dewey Albinson, Andrew Bakalar, Helen Bakalar, Mary Bastis, Anna Chovanec, Susan Cupka, Anna Dargay, George Dargay, Carrie Finstrom, Mrs. John Grega, Mamie Groscost, N. A. Johnson, Arthur Kerrick, Elizabeth Kieferle, John Lucas, F. B. Matlach, Mrs. J. S. Mičatek, Mrs. Magnus Olson, Elizabeth Pehousek, Anna Petro, Florence Rowles, Margaret Rubshik, Andrew Sabako, Susan Sabako, Anna Sabol, Rose Shafar, Thomas Shafar, Susan Shingler, Mrs. Franklin Vanek, Josie Verabec, Mrs. Franklin G. Wallace, Michael C. Zipoy, and Josephine Zipoy.

ROSCOE MACY, *State Supervisor*
Minnesota WPA Writers' Project

The
Bohemian
Flats

Seventy-nine Steps Down

Of the old Bohemian Flats, little is left to attract the notice of passers-by. Many other things catch the eye as one comes upon the Washington Avenue bridge from the downtown-Minneapolis end. Ahead and below meanders the Mississippi, its gray-green surface mottled here and there with purple pools of oil discharged from passing motor craft. At this point the river, just beginning to gather substantial volume, is scarcely a quarter of a mile wide. In the course of centuries it has cut a miniature gorge for its channel, with high bluffs on both sides extending almost from the Falls of St. Anthony above the bridge to the mouth of the Minnesota River a few miles downstream.

At the opposite end of the bridge naked limestone cliffs jut steeply upward from the river's edge. Crowning the bluff are the varicolored buildings of the University of Minnesota. Southward from the campus, where the river bends around a grassy bank, a cluster of houseboats ride at anchor.

On the west shore of the river, beneath the Washington Avenue bridge, is the Municipal Barge Terminal, piled with heaps of coal and scrap iron and flanked by strings of scows, barges that from the bridge above appear less enormous than they actually are, and an occasional tugboat or an old stern-wheeler. On this side the bluff stands perhaps three or four hundred feet back from the river, the ground sloping off gradually in a series of benches from the base of the cliff to the water's edge. Two of these shelves are well defined, one a few feet higher than the other, and they have been known almost since the beginning of Minneapolis as the upper and lower levee, or the Bohemian Flats. They are reached from Washington Avenue by descending a rude wooden stairway of seventy-nine steps, which dips down the face of the bluff alongside the west bridge approach.

Cut off from the city by the river at its doorstep and the steep bluffs behind, the settlement of the Bohemian Flats was born and grew up in a unique geographic and cultural isolation. Until only yesterday life in this little pocket had something of a pastoral quality that contrasted sharply with the city traffic humming and roaring across the bridge above it. For more than half a century a picturesque and hard-working colony of men and women from the Old World clung tenaciously to their tiny plots of ground beneath the cliffs. Their manners and customs, and indeed the very atmosphere of the place, had a foreign flavor, indestructibly appealing.

The Bohemian Flats is a good many years past its heyday. Where once were upwards of a hundred homes there are now but fourteen, and of the onetime five hundred or more inhabitants scarcely fifty remain. Land laws and the needs of a growing city are inexorable forces. They have erased all but a fraction of the original village. It may be that the present small remnant of the old settlement will be allowed to stay on unmolested, or it may not. In any event the story of the Bohemian Flats ought to be recorded while it is still traceable, for most of that story will soon be lost with the memories of those who can tell it.

The settlement on the lower flat is already only a memory, with the barge terminal's pyramids of coal for a marker, but the plank stairway still leads down to the upper flat, what is left of it, on the downstream side of the bridge. There was little enough space there in the old days for a house and a garden and a patch of grass inside a picket fence. There is less now. Almost as if they sensed a common danger the fourteen houses stand huddled together close up under the bluff.

But the strange charm is there yet. Front doors open unexpectedly onto bits of lawn that in summer are green and tidy, with flowers bursting into color around the roots of

[2

ancient trees. An old man comes down the hill. Possibly he is a former resident of the Flats who cannot accustom himself to the taste of chlorine in the city water. He opens the suitcase he is carrying, takes out some mason jars, fills them with "good water" from Carrie Finstrom's pump, then starts the slow walk back up "to the city." In winter icicles hang from crevices in the limestone cliff. A coal truck moves up the road from the terminal, spattering lumps from an overfull load as the driver takes a sharp turn, and a woman with a loose sweater over a calico dress uses a mop handle to rake the coal outside her stoop into a pile, until there is enough to fill her scuttle. In the spring the river rises, but never beyond the sea wall. And in the fall the smell of pickles, sauerkraut, and crushed grapes comes drifting from the kitchen windows of the Flats, and folks from over the hill join the villagers in hunting mushrooms.

Today progress has come to the Flats. "We're getting a new oil burner," a child sings out to a neighbor. There are water mains and electricity and telephone service for those who want them and can afford them. Milk and groceries and mail are delivered to the doors, and the Flats people no longer distrust doctors. Discreet outhouses are still tucked away in back yards and woodsheds, but modern automobiles are occasionally parked at the curbs. Progress has come, but it is progress in small things. There is still an air of impermanence there beside the river and the great buildings of the university set solid against the sky.

Long ago, when the Bohemian Flats and the university were both young, Old Main, the single university building, turned its back to the humble squatters on the other side of the river. Near in space, the university and the Flats were far apart in spirit. Now, however, the two communities are old. Both have seen their children grow up and leave them. They are old neighbors, though set in their separate ways, and the nodding acquaintance of years has grown into a friendship not easily or often expressed, probably not much thought about. Slowly the university has turned its face around, and now looks almost straight down to where the Flats look up.

In these declining years of the Flats Franklin G. Wallace, of the university faculty, and his wife have taken the final step in the tentative association of the past. They have just finished their fourth year as residents there. Though Mrs. Wallace has written about it as "the adventure of riverbank life," it means more than adventure to her, for she says with feeling that she and her husband will never again be content to live on a regular street in a row of houses, with only another row of houses across from them.

When the Wallaces came to the university they went house-hunting below the bridge. They had been fascinated by the seventy-nine wooden steps leading down to the village, and they were attracted by what they found at the foot of the stairway for the same reason that brought many of the early pioneers there—because it was beautiful and interesting and inexpensive.

"When we looked up a little side street," Mrs. Wallace relates, "and saw a deserted and run-down cottage there with a big but mussy side yard running up the bank, we realized that if we were game for it this might well be the answer to our housing problem. When we inquired about renting, we were told right away that there was no running water on the Flats and that no sewer ran down to that level. But we felt that there were many things to make up for this." So the Wallaces rented the old Bender place, a few feet up the street from the immaculate, gray-painted house of eighty-year-old Mrs. Bastis.

Mrs. Wallace is pleased with all that followed. "By the time we had got the windows mended and the doors hung, the wide-board floors sanded and smoothed, and paint spread generally both inside and out, we turned our attention to the yard. After clearing out the old coal box and the piled-up rubbish we could see that the yard had a beautiful shape, being terraced on three levels as it slopes up toward the bluff. When that first spring came we planted grass. As the leaves came out, we found ourselves with an unbelievably lovely yard."

In the kitchen they set up an old-fashioned range, that

"never goes out, except accidentally, all winter long." The kitchen range and the oil heater in the living room keep the house warm during the cold months at a small cost for fuel. "We got our water across the street," Mrs. Wallace says, "from a spring that the neighbors assured us had been used since the earliest times and was thought to be very healthful. We used to carry water intensively by bucket on Saturday afternoons, filling a big tank. Unluckily the summer after we moved, in the spring became contaminated with gas and was no longer usable. This meant hauling our water from Miss Finstrom's pump down the street. The pump is a real community center but it is quite a distance away from us. Something had to be done, and finally the city was persuaded to do it. A line of city water was run from the hydrant lines at the barge terminal across to the corner of our street. Three houses had the water put in then. Of course, no one is tempted to use very much, since there are no drains and it must be carried out by hand."

The Wallaces like their Flats neighbors, and Mrs. Bastis and the Shafars and Mrs. Kieferle and Mrs. Petro speak well of the Wallaces. Though they do not all get together often, Mrs. Wallace says there is a strong community spirit in the settlement. Once she and her husband gave a party in their yard, and "one of the men remarked that it was the first time he could remember their all getting together—and it took a newcomer to do it." Interest in the river traffic is a common bond. "During a day in summer we often see several stern-wheelers with their trains of barges, each whistling as it comes into view where the river bends below the houseboat anchorage. The village children can always tell you whether it is the *Huck Finn* or the *Patrick J. Hurley* or some other one."

Like the first of the Flats dwellers, the Wallaces do much of their summer cooking outdoors, over a fireplace built of river stones. And with their neighbors they share a possessive affection for the Flats, and an uneasiness about the future.

"In these four years we have watched the march of commerce that seems to threaten us," Mrs. Wallace remarks. "The coal area is to be greatly increased, and just during the last year we have been closed in even more by the construction of an oil terminal downstream from us. There is also talk, up in the city, of moving the bridge. Whether the whole section will finally be bought up or whether the few little houses will remain as landmarks it is impossible to say."

The women who meet at the pump have lived with this perennial problem so long that some of them declare themselves indifferent to it. "I'd like to make a change," Mrs. Kieferle admits, rocking while she mends. "For the girls' sake mostly, but for myself too." Her daughter, a pretty girl in her twenties, agrees from the ironing board. "It can't come too soon for me." The Flats are all right, says Carrie Finstrom, but she adds that the outskirts of the city would be nice.

At one time or another most of the Flats women mention the conveniences they could enjoy if they moved up "to the city." But they rarely move, and most of them dread the day when they may have to. Mrs. Petro, who came to America fifty-four years ago, shakes her head. "If it's true about the bridge I can't figure it out. I see when I ride on the streetcar to town no flowers. No flowers at all." Mrs. Sabol, whose son-in-law teases her because of "the way I talk, getting my English words all mixed," looks at the apple tree in her yard, then up at the bridge. Her smile is not quite a smile, and she shrugs her shoulders. "I like it here, working in my garden." "We've been hearing about the bridge for so many years," one of the two Shafar sisters says, "that we're ready. Anyway we won't have to move. Maybe Mrs. Sabol will, she's so close to the bridge, but we're far enough away." Mrs. Bastis says nothing. Her children have suggested that it is time for her to come up from the Flats and live with them. She is making up her mind and it is not easy.

During the time that the Wallaces have been on the Flats the Shafar sisters tried moving away. "We went to live with my sister in Duluth," one of them explains. "It seemed like a good idea when we left, the three of us being together."

But they were so homesick they could hardly wait until spring to return home. As she remembers that mistake, Miss Shafar's glance takes in the whole of her freshly mopped kitchen. "I'd rather have an arm- or a leg-ache than a heart-ache," she says.

The Shafars' return was felt in university circles across the river. While the sisters were gone university friends of the Wallaces, Mr. and Mrs. Magnus Olson, rented their house. Like the Wallaces they found in the village below the bridge what seemed to them the good life. When the Shafar sisters hurried back home the Olsons had to go up again "to the city." Mrs. Kieferle says sympathetically that Mrs. Olson almost cried, and Carrie Finstrom still thinks it was a pity there was no place on the Flats for the Olsons to stay.

This is the Bohemian Flats today. Twenty years ago, before the city acted to clear away the settlement on the lower flat, before the villagers were scattered over the hill into the anonymous streets they never cared for, the Flats were different only in degree. There were many more little houses then and many more people in them, more children and dogs and poultry, more jolly Slovak feasts, more Bibles read in the Czech language that their owners had neither the heart nor the time to forget.

In smaller measure it is all there yet, on the remnant of the upper flat. Curiously too the past is repeating itself. River traffic to Minneapolis has been revived. "This is industrial property now," one resident declares. "Yes," another agrees, echoing words spoken sixty years ago. "Yes, we must hold on to it. It will bring a good price pretty soon."

Meanwhile a new generation of Minneapolitans stops on the bridge to look down on the romantic jumble of the Bohemian Flats. Most of them take it for granted. It has been there as long as they can remember. Some of them who recall bits of old folks' talk wonder when the Flats began and what they were like before now and what happened to the rest of the families on the edge of the river. Even the old folks, those who live up "in the city," do not know all about those things.

Settlers in Bohemia

Seventy-five years ago the area now known as the Bohemian Flats was one of the many scenic spots for which Minnesota was famous as far south as New Orleans. The magnificent sweep of the Mississippi at this point, as it wound past the beautiful Falls of St. Anthony on its way to Mendota and beyond, the cliffs rising sheer and bare on the east shore, the shading trees on the west, interspersed with shrubbery and wild flowers—all gave to the Flats a rich beauty that was fully appreciated by the early settlers who made their homes there.

An English scholar, George Tuthill Barrett, who traveled through Minneapolis in the early sixties, was struck by the primeval freshness and charm of the place. In his *Letters from Canada and the U.S.A.*, published in 1865, he wrote: "Along the edge of the cliff, I sat until the sun went down. It was one of the prettiest scenes I have met with on this continent. The river ran beneath at the bottom of a narrow gorge, its banks wooded to the water's edge and dotted with an occasional house that peeped forth from the dense, dark foliage."

No official record of the original settlement of the Flats exists. According to the statement of Thomas Shafar, who worked his way up the river to Minneapolis in 1869 and lived along the riverbank for many years, a Danish couple was the first family on the Flats. In describing the two Mr. Shafar recalled vividly that "he was always fishing and she was always washing and scrubbing." Since the little settlement was first known as the Danish Flats, it is probable that the two were joined by some of the other immigrants of Scandinavian origin who were pouring into the Northwest at that time.

Paul Gyllstrom (1869–1924), a pioneer Minneapolis newspaperman, remarks in his memoirs that the Bohemians "must have made their initial appearance about 1869 or 1870." In a pamphlet issued by the Saint Emmanuel Slovak Lutheran Church of Minneapolis it is stated that the Slovaks began to arrive here in 1880 and to settle along the riverbank. The further addition of a dozen Irish and two German settlers and an unknown number of Polish and French immigrants gave the little river colony from its very beginning a truly cosmopolitan flavor.

In the *Northwest Magazine* of July 1887 the settlement is described as follows:

"Not far below the St. Anthony Falls and in the Minneapolis city limits, you can see from the bluff on either side a curious little village, low down by the water's edge. It is, in fact, two villages, for the settlement is divided into two parts by the Mississippi River, and each occupies a shelving flat of land that extends out not much above the water's level. There are no streets. The houses are dropped about in a strange fashion and in irregular lines, with no reference to a roadway or the point of compass known as the Flats. They are wholly wooden houses and mostly one story high, untouched by any paint other than that of frosts, sun marks and storm stains. They look dingy and forlorn in the extreme. Their contrast with the high mills and elevators and the huge city blocks above them and in plain sight, adds to the feature of picturesqueness which they present, while the white foam of the falls and the lofty descent from the river above, puts in a touch that fulfills the most unique requirement of a painter's canvass."

"Minneapolis started down here," says an old settler who came to the Flats sixty-five years ago. "There were little boats on the river, and the breeze and the beautiful banks. Everyone had flowers growing from their window boxes or around the trees. It was just like a park, and on Sundays all the people used to come down to have picnics and take pictures and walk around the little houses."

Of course Minneapolis started at the Falls of St. Anthony, upstream from the Flats, and several years before settlement began on the Flats. When Thomas Shafar found the Danish couple there in 1869, St. Anthony on the east side of the river and Minneapolis, its slightly younger neighbor on the west side, had already been incorporated as cities with a combined population of some eighteen thousand. Three years later they were united.

In this period after the Civil War, the Minneapolis–St. Anthony community outgrew its frontier beginnings. It was a city that had meant to get ahead since Franklin Steele in 1848 built his dam and sawmill, and it was now well on its way. A flood of immigration was moving in over the surrounding country. Trade and industry were expanding from a solid base of lumber and flour. There was already an aristocracy of so-called old families, and the stamp of their New England enterprise and culture was making a permanent impression. The Minneapolis press did not hesitate to call St. Paul "the way station" and itself "the seat of destiny."

It was indeed a thriving and aggressive young city to which both Thomas Shafar and William Watts Folwell, new president of the state university, came in 1869. A little more than a decade later Folwell had reason to fear that "a solid phalanx of mills and factories will reach from the Falls to the University hill" and that the "elevators storing the grain for the great flour mills will loom against our front." But in those first years Folwell, up on the east-side bluff, and the immigrants, down on the west-side Flats, were well outside the pushing center of the city.

Old Main then stood, Folwell reported, "in a distant suburb." It looked upriver toward the Falls and the faded elegance of the Winslow House, and on the green lawn of the campus grazed a herd of fine cows, a gift from nearby citizens that gave "much pleasure and profit to the students." And while President Folwell was complaining to the board of regents in 1870 that Old Main, heated by wood-burning stoves and lighted by lamps, was "about as ill adapted to the purposes it was serving as any that could be easily devised," a St. Anthony journalist was examining the university's social tone. It was not so snobbish as it seemed, he said. On the contrary, it was "healthy, genuine, hearty, well-bred." But, he added cautiously, "what it will become in the future is uncertain."

Nobody was greatly concerned about the social tone of that section of Minneapolis across the river from the university. Like the scattered suburb around the campus, it was enough that it was a good place to live. Washington Avenue, Paul Gyllstrom remembered, stretched down to the river from Seven Corners—an unpaved street then, with wooden sidewalks bordered by picket fences and pleasant lawns where lilacs and apple trees blossomed in the spring. Southtown boys swam in the river at a spot where a strip of white sand followed the Mississippi's contour. Directly below what was in 1886 to become the site of the Washington Avenue bridge, there was "a wonderful slope of green" down among the oaks and the hickory and butternut trees.

The early Bohemian Flats settlers drifted to the riverbank to live because most of them had little money, and land rent was cheap along the upper and lower levee. On the lower tier, along the river, a lot large enough for a shanty and a small back yard could be rented for from fifty cents to two dollars a month. On the upper tier ground rent ranged from fifteen to twenty-five dollars a year.

While rents were low, there is evidence that those who bought homes on the upper levee sometimes paid a good round sum for the privilege. It is also true that wishful speculation occasionally influenced the more affluent of the settlers. "They bought a lot here for five hundred dollars, when they could have got one up above, in the city, for less," an old resident relates. "But they chose this place because the real-estate men told them it was to be the navigation center of the Northwest in a few years. They were the first settlers on the upper levee, but it was a great picnic ground then."

That some of the immigrants were induced by real-estate promoters to make unwise investments in land is attested to by several witnesses. "When people moved down here they paid five hundred dollars for every one of the lots, and they got cheated. There wasn't even any ground. It was all just limestone chips from all the quarries around here. This place was filled with quarries. The settlers had to bring mud up from the river and haul down loads of dirt and fertilizer, until finally the weather washed some better land into the hollow." Another tells that he paid "four hundred and fifty dollars for a hole and filled it up with dirt at ten cents a load. That took many weeks. The city brought dirt from the streets, but my next-door neighbor stopped it because of horse manure in the sweepings. It was all topped off with sand."

The houses on the upper levee were spaced farther apart than the shanties on the lower levee beside the river. Most of them had garden lots where the householders raised cucumbers, parsley, cabbage, and celery, and tended at least one apple tree each. Everyone grew flowers, even on the lower flat. The interior of the houses shone with whitewash. Those on the lower levee had no basements or second stories.

Many of the immigrants had come to this country with the intention of making their "pile" and then returning in comparative wealth to their families in the old country. Once settled in their new homes, however, they decided that freedom tasted sweet. "We heard that when you worked in America you got money for it," a black-eyed Czech mother relates. "We worked there in the baron's fields for the scraps left behind. Our tiny piece of land we had bought with many generations of lifetime labor. When the landowner said 'Come to my fields tomorrow' the men had to go, even though their own crops needed work. If they didn't work fast enough they were whipped. If they refused to go they were jailed. The baron gave them a few pennies, never more than twenty cents, and many times their own crops spoiled." So most of the Flats immigrants remained here, found work in the mills and the factories "on the hill," as they called the city proper, and, when they could, invited their families or relatives to join them in their new homes on this side of the ocean.

Singly and in couples, others made the journey from Central Europe to the bank of the alien river. New Czech and Slovak homes went up beside those of their compatriots. To them, too, freedom tasted sweet, and in time the river was no longer alien. "In evening hours," a Minneapolitan remembered many years later, "there was a most friendly glow in the lights of the Bohemian Flats community. Its general appearance was like that of a little fishing village in some Old World seaport, minus, of course, the ships that go out to sea. It had the charm of an old picture."

On a day in the 1880's the Connemaras, a band of thirty or more immigrants from Ireland, of all ages, arrived in Minneapolis. They were pitifully poor, and to aggravate their misery they could not make themselves understood, since they spoke only Gaelic. They attracted a great deal of attention as they straggled down from the railway station in a long, tired line, their belongings wrapped in bright cloths. "The Connemaras have come! The Connemaras have come!" people would shout as the new arrivals passed through their neighborhood.

Weary and bewildered, the Connemaras huddled together at the rim of the hill above the Flats and waited for divine Providence to come to their aid. An Irishwoman in the neighborhood, a Mrs. John Fallon, took them in hand and distributed them among her Irish friends, while the men began to build a communal lodging on the Flats for the newcomers. With driftwood dragged from the river they made a roomy dwelling close to the shore, and all the Connemaras moved in. Makeshift beds were constructed for the adults, while the children slept on bundles of straw on the floor. Cooking and other domestic work was done on a communal basis. The men found work in the mills and factories nearby. One by one each family acquired its own shanty and moved into it, until eventually the community house was empty. It was then torn down and used for fuel. The Conne-

13]

maras lived along the riverbank for a long time, joined now and then by a few new members and now and then losing some of the original party.

Swedes, Danes, and Germans also came to live there, but the little settlement developed as a predominantly Slavic village. Best known as the Bohemian Flats, it has also been called, in the course of its variegated history, Little Bohemia, the Connemara Patch, Little Ireland, Little Lithuania, and the Danish Flats. Artists and newspapermen named it the Cabbage Patch; and in the spring, when the river overflowed its banks and the dwellers of the lower flat poled scows from window to window, gathering up featherbeds, ducks, and children, the news reporters appropriately christened it Little Venice. In the prosaic surveys and plat books of the city, it is known simply as the Washington Avenue Addition.

Construction of the Northern Pacific bridge, ca. 1885 (Emil Hilgarde photo, Minnesota Historical Society)

Spectators on the Washington Avenue bridge, ca. 1885 (Minnesota Historical Society)

Children playing on the Flats, ca. 1895 (M. Eva McIntyre photo, Minneapolis History Collection, Minneapolis Public Library and Information Center)

Street scene, ca. 1895 (M. Eva McIntyre photo, Minneapolis History Collection, Minneapolis Public Library and Information Center)

Looking toward the Northern Pacific bridge, ca. 1895 (M. Eva McIntyre photo, Minneapolis History Collection, Minneapolis Public Library and Information Center)

Sophie Sheffel, born near Prague in 1882, the youngest of eight children. The photographer identified her as "the bright Bohemian girl"; she later became a nurse. (Minnesota Historical Society)

Holy Emmanuel Slovak Lutheran Church, 101 Cooper Street, ca. 1900
(Minneapolis Journal photo, Minnesota Historical Society)

The University of Minnesota from the Flats, 1903. Buildings, from left to right: School of Mines, Old Main, Library (Burton Hall), Animal Laboratory, Hall of Mechanic Arts (Eddy Hall), Anatomical Building, Medical Building (Wulling Hall) (Louis Sweet photo, Minnesota Historical Society)

Catching wood, ca. 1905 (Minnesota Historical Society)

Flats under Northern Pacific bridge at flood time, ca. 1910; Minneapolis
Brewing Company at upper left (Minnesota Historical Society)

First commercial shipment to arrive at the new Minneapolis Municipal River Terminal, south of the Washington Avenue bridge, July 18, 1917. It consisted of $90,000 worth of John Deere plows from Moline, Illinois. (Minnesota Historical Society)

Municipal River Terminal, May 1924 (Minnesota Historical Society)

Street scene, probably 1928 (Alvin E. Kairies photo, Hennepin County Historical Society)

Street scene, probably 1928 (Alvin E. Kairies photo, Hennepin County Historical Society)

Mrs. Anna Chipka, Flats resident, June 2, 1929 (Minneapolis History Collection, Minneapolis Public Library and Information Center)

Paul Bozonie, sixteen years old, repairs his canoe on Cooper Street, 1929. Helping him are Joe Chipka and John Zustiak; Mary Chipka and Sally Andrusko look on. (Hennepin County Historical Society)

Pump on the Flats, ca. 1935 (Minnesota Historical Society)

Milk cellar, ca. 1936 (Minnesota Historical Society)

Steps to the Flats, ca. 1938 (Minnesota Historical Society)

**Municipal Coal Dock, north of the Washington Avenue bridge, ca. 1945
(Minnesota Historical Society)**

Municipal River Terminal, ca. 1950 (Minnesota Historical Society)

Life on the Flats

Rude indeed were the homes and surroundings of the early settlers of the Flats. Appropriating the logs, blocks, and boards that floated downstream from the sawmills, they constructed their shacks. Holes in the lumber they patched with anything they could find—tin cans hammered flat, or laths, or thin boards. Sometimes the shacks were covered with tar paper. Most of them were very small and without foundations. An old resident of the city describes the homes of the early village as "so small they looked like little cigar boxes on a stage street. They were crowded so close together that if you stepped out of the front door you were standing on your neighbor's doorstep." In time, and as soon as their means allowed, the settlers added attics, parlors, and extra bedrooms. In time, too, color overspread and hid the drab exteriors. Fences, sheds, and houses received shiny coats of blue, yellow, red, green, or pink paint. Gay flowerpots and embroidered curtains appeared in the windows, and the little colony blossomed in the brightest colors.

The people built their houses along the three main streets of the village, all of which ran parallel with the river. Rent was highest on Mill Street, on the aristocratic upper levee where the settlers paid about twenty-five dollars a year for their "lease," as they called their rent payment. Along Cooper Street, farther down, it cost eighteen dollars a year, and about fifteen dollars a year on Wood Street, along the riverbank. The early settlers cannot remember to whom they paid their rent, except that it was to "some lawyer."

The quarries that operated adjacent to the Flats had left portions of it covered with limestone chips, but the settlers, undaunted, dragged rich black mud from the river bottom and covered their little plots with it, and soon beds of parsley, celery, garlic, and poppy seed turned every back yard into a garden, with bright cliff stones bordering the walks. Poultry, rabbits, and dogs multiplied in amiable confusion.

Many of the settlers, especially those who had larger houses, took in boarders. Sometimes as many as twelve single men, workers in the mills, boarded in one house. Some of them bought their own groceries and paid the landlady two dollars a month for their cooking, washing, and sleeping room. Others, in groups, preferred to divide the cost of a month's meat and groceries equally among themselves and pay the landlady two dollars a month for services. Unmarried women supported themselves by doing domestic work in the homes of others. Some obtained employment in the larger boardinghouses "on the hill," where they frequently found husbands among the boarders and moved back to the Flats to set up homes of their own.

About thirty years ago a large brick apartment house was built on the Flats. Originally intended as a rooming house for brewery workers it later sheltered a dozen Slovak families and their boarders. Because of its size it was frequently used as a social center and numerous ice cream socials, made lighthearted by old country music and dances, were held there.

From the 1880's on, the Bohemian Flats enjoyed a steady growth. About 1886 a Slovak named Joseph Kokesh put up a small, square building and opened a grocery store. He ran the business through the best years of the settlement's history and left the Flats a well-to-do merchant.

The men found employment in the lumberyards, sawmills, and flour mills near the settlement. Since the usual pay at the lumberyards was a dollar and a half a day, work at the Washburn, Pillsbury, and other flour mills, which paid two dollars a day, was preferred. "Those two dollars appealed to them as much as ten or twenty dollars would now," an old settler declares. "Many people who had come with the idea of saving money and buying land in Europe changed their minds and decided not to go back. They thought conditions here were so much better than in their homeland."

Some of the men went to work in the coopering shops, for cooperage was an industry that was expanding to meet the demand for flour barrels, butter tubs, and pickle kegs. Others were employed as laborers by the railroads and the streetcar company. An old Scandinavian settler eked out a living by fishing through the ice during the winter months, smoking his catch and selling it up "on the hill." When a pickle factory was opened nearby some of the village girls obtained jobs sorting cucumbers.

Children too young to work in the city found jobs waiting for them in their own back yard—the river. They gathered the billets of wood, mill ends, "dead heads" (entire logs), and other sawmill waste that came floating downstream. In the hectic days of logging—one of the chief industries of early Minnesota—the river was full of logs from early spring until the first of July. The yard behind each house was filled with wood piles. Some of the wood was used for household fuel and the remainder was sold. Old men no longer agile enough for factory work joined the youngsters along the riverbank. These logging operations were described in detail by a writer who witnessed them in 1887.

"Of the harvest, from April to November, an almost uninterrupted stream comes. Slabs, shingles, strips, blocks, boards and sometimes entire logs can be seen hurrying down the river, which is quite rapid at this point, and it is a very novel spectacle to see the way they manage to secure the valuable flotsam that the waters are always bringing to them at their door. Everyone riding to Minneapolis from St. Paul can see them on the car from the windows as they ride over. They have built from dozens of points on the shore . . . out of their own gathered material, long platforms placed upon rude, low piers, on which they wade to reach the current. With crooked sticks or pronged instruments they grasp the stick of wood that comes in reach, and land it usually, with

17]

much dexterity, upon the platform, then wait for the next one.

"Sometimes they don't get it and it goes to the next wood fisher below. Some sticks go out of reach of each platform, but hardly any go out of reach of the whole group, for they all gather large quantities and, so nearly alike, it would seem as if the river, in spirit of benevolence, sought to do its duty by the owners of each platform.

"Platforms are of various lengths. Some go only a few feet from the shore, and some appear to be several rods in length. They are strongly placed, and when piles at the end are too much in the way, other piles are made in the rear of it at different distances, clear back to the shore.

"Little boys and girls, ten to twelve years old, are kept fishing for wood and taking it into the land. When they gather it, they are quite willing to step out, and are apparently obliged to do so, into the shallow water itself for the prizes they seek. You see them sitting at the edge of the platform, or running about the shore with bare legs, and ready for any water emergency that might occur. This picturesque labor brings more wood than they use, and they have large quantities to sell. Old men, who can't work at trades, make a business all year long. One year, an old man took three hundred cords of wood from the river. It should be worth three dollars a cord at least, he figured, no matter in what shape or irregularity it comes. At any rate, he could make a respectable salary. . . .

"In December, the river platforms are all frozen in, and the children skate between them on the ice. The sawmills cease to send down their wood at that season, but you see a few teamsters driving to the edge of the east bluff to load up wood that a couple of men below lift up from a series of platforms built on the side of the bluff for that purpose. The product is handled carefully, although it is clutched from the river's bed, for they have gotten it by hard work and a lot of patience."

Wood was not the only thing that came floating down the Mississippi. Oranges and bananas, dumped into the river by wholesale fruit houses, sometimes bobbed about in the current. "We saw a child eating one of those bananas from the river when we first came," an old resident recalls, "and we thought he would die. The whole place was in a panic until we found out that everyone ate them here. Until I came to America I had never seen a banana."

At first almost every immigrant owned a cow, which was kept in its tiny "pasture" by means of a fence made of sticks pushed into the ground and reinforced with vines and saplings. The cows frequently broke through the fences and wandered about the village. As other immigrants came, seeking land on which to build homes, the pastures were sacrificed. A Slovak woman named Karitish, who lived on the lower flat, then established a dairy. She kept her seven cows in a cave in the cliff and, accompanied by her small son, delivered the milk each morning and evening, hauling the two twenty-gallon cans up and down the streets. She sold the milk for five cents a quart. Her husband, who managed the business when his wife was ill, found it simpler to lead a cow through the settlement and produce the milk to order on each customer's doorstep. Eventually Mrs. Karitish lost her customers to the milk companies "on the hill."

European domestic habits persisted for a long time among the residents of the Flats. The old-country method of washing clothes in a handy stream was carried over without change to the banks of the Mississippi. A pioneer resident of the village has explained the method. "First the clothes were soaked, then boiled for an hour or two. Next day we took them out, hauled them to the river, and paddled them with a wide stick. Then we rinsed them over and over until they were snowy white. Unless there was a baby in the house we had enough clothes so we had to wash only once a month. Usually one woman in the neighborhood had an iron. We starched our blouses and she ironed them so the sleeves stood out pretty, for church. She did that in exchange for a bunch of vegetables or some dried mushrooms or berries." Another resident remembers that "some of the women soaked their washing in a huge wooden barrel and covered them with ashes for about a week. They came out white that way too." Rugs were usually taken down to the river, scrubbed on a wooden bench, carefully rinsed, and placed on the rocks to dry.

Gradually washing was transferred to the homes, where washboards took the place of rough stones. Barrels were set out to catch the soft rain water, since the water from the springs in the limestone cliffs was too hard. On Mondays the sight of sturdy, barefoot women bending over their wooden tubs announced that it was washday. Gay aprons and shirts and blouses, each with its touch of native needlework, hung on lines stretched from tree to tree almost down to the water's edge.

On the lower flat drinking water and water for general household use were obtained from the springs in the cliff or more often from the numerous wells in the villagers' yards. Many of these wells were sunk deep below the level of the river, a former resident declares, and the water was very cold and good. These were old-style windlass wells, the full bucket being raised by a hand crank. The shafts were lined sometimes with wood and sometimes with river stones, and to keep out both dirt and romping youngsters a well was often enclosed with wooden siding and a roof, with the bucket sitting on a shelf inside the door. Around 1900 several cases of typhoid fever among the settlers caused the city health authorities to condemn most of these wells. To take their place a hydrant line from the city mains was run down to the village.

Every kitchen had its range and baking was a daily affair. In summer, to escape the discomfort of indoor baking, the women gathered boulders and built long outdoor ovens. These ovens were considered community property and were in daily use. As was the custom in their native land they mixed rye flour and a little lard or other fat with caraway seeds and homemade yeast, kneaded the dough into enormous loaves on large, flat rocks, and let the "black bread with little seeds in him" bake for hours in the hot oven. When baked, the loaves were pulled out of the oven with long poles and allowed to cool. From the leftover dough the women made "little figures of men" for the children.

In time the homely rock oven and even the kitchen range gave way somewhat to commercial baking. A baker's wagon began to make the rounds daily, calling the women to the cart with Slovak tunes played on an accordion. "The bread is not so good," the women admitted, "but it gives us more time."

The immigrant's diet was as strange and interesting to outsiders as his other Old World habits. In the fall the women went forth to gather huge supplies of the mushrooms that grew so plentifully along the riverbank and at the foot of the cliffs. They returned with washtubs, wooden kegs, clothes baskets, and potato sacks filled with the plants. Grandmothers, recalling mushroom time in the old country, squatted in their yards and spread the plants out to dry or prepared them for cooking. Most of the Flats dwellers preferred to dry the mushrooms rather than can them, since canning was a process strange to them and, as they probably thought, too complicated and expensive. An old grandmother, speaking of mushroom time in Europe, says, "When we were children we used to go in the fall and pick them wild to sell. A little we saved for the holidays. Most we took to market to trade for flour and bread." Over here, though, the money the men were earning in the mills and factories made it generally possible to keep the mushrooms for home use.

Cooking was an art to which the Czech and Slovak housewives gave skilled and loving attention. From the few simple staples that composed the mainstay of their diet they created an ingenious variety of palatable dishes. Several of their recipes may be found in the last section of this book.

Potatoes were cooked in at least thirty-five different ways. There was potato strudel—cooked potatoes to which flour was added, rolled until stiff, sprinkled with butter and cinnamon, baked, and sliced; and there were potato noodles—potatoes cooked and "mushed," with flour added, cut into artistic designs, and covered with butter and poppy seed; and all the other potato dishes. Cheese was also popular, and

Bohemian cheese was rated as "better than the Swiss." Butter was made from goat's milk. Many a Flats dweller kept a goat tied to a stake in the back yard. Cabbage was another indispensable article of diet, and the Czechs considered their cabbage better than that of the Slovaks and the Germans— "sweet, white, and tender." Fish cooked in a variety of ways was also common on the immigrant's table.

Sauerkraut was still another food held in high esteem by the people of the Flats, and the source of much good-natured rivalry among the different nationalities. The Germans declared their kraut was the best but the Czechs contested the claim. To all—German, Czech, or Slovak—sauerkraut was a national dish and no meal was complete without it. On religious fast days, when meat could not be served, the housewives flavored the gravy with sauerkraut juice. On Christmas and other festive occasions huge bowls of kraut formed the principal dish of the meal.

A species of grape that grew wild in the vicinity of the Flats was gathered for wine and jellies. The *palina* plant, a European wormwood transplanted to this country by immigrants, was gathered in the woods each fall, bunched, and hung in the lofts or over the kitchen cupboards to dry.

Two of the largest breweries of the city were located not far from the Flats. The late Thomas Shafar, who came to the Flats in the same year that William Watts Folwell became president of the university and who is believed to have been the first Bohemian on the Minneapolis police force, related that "when the saloons on the hill closed on Sunday many of the early residents of the city came down to the breweries. The Flats people would buy a keg of beer and take it down to one of the little shacks. Sometimes the parties became a bit rough. The immigrants had been held down for so long that some of them went wild over their freedom. Of course the beer helped a lot. By evening they'd often be full and fighting. Sometimes when I went down to quiet the place, the women came out after me with teakettles full of scalding water." A similar explanation of the revels is given by another former resident of the Flats, who says that some of the village men "had been under the yoke so long before they came here that, finding such freedom and all, it was hard on them. They frisked around like young calves that won't stop 'til they break their legs."

When winter settled on the Flats each little dwelling seemed embedded in a snowdrift, and the settlement stood out starkly against the background of frosted cliffs and frozen river. On days when it was too cold to leave the house, the plaintive strains of the family fiddle kept the housewife company while she prepared the evening supper or sat contentedly by the loom, making rugs out of bright rags.

The children skated in the squares made by the piers of the wood gatherers, when the river was frozen hard enough. Slovak fathers made skates of wood with a thick strip of metal forming the runner. Rope was used to strap the skates to the feet.

From the parted curtains of their small windows the villagers could see the long white hill extending from Cedar Avenue down to the river. When a man on the upper flat built an enormous bobsled and began to rent it to university students for sledding parties, the settlers often rented it too. Two or three times an evening they would slide down the hill, scattering all over the bank when the sled stopped suddenly. Coasting eventually became an established sport in the village. To indulge in this recreation almost as many outsiders came down to the village in the winter as in the summer, when excursion boats plowed the river and the mossy banks shaded by the bluffs invited picnickers.

Spring meant floods to the lower flat. As the ice went out the river in its headlong haste would overflow its banks, and the low-lying village was in its path. Seeing the water rise, the villagers would appear at their kitchen doors and call to their neighbors "It looks like spring!" By the time the river rose to the stoops, they had begun to haul their beds to the homes of neighbors living on higher land, or to the Sunday school, or up to the caves abandoned by the breweries.

If the water began to flow into the houses they had more

work on their hands. Clothing, dishes, and furniture had to be moved quickly. With placid stoicism some of the residents refused to make any precautionary move until they were forced to wade up to their doors. Rubber boots were kept for such occasions as this, and old scows were once more put to use. A housewife whose home was on the hill above the Flats remembers the scene. "As soon as the water got too high the women would go out in these boats and start paddling around. I remember wishing, when I was young, that I could live down there so I could be right in the mess." Most of the settlers on the lower level had boats, since they were the first to be cut off from the rest of the colony by floods. Rickety bridges of narrow planks set on blocks of wood and stakes provided a dry crossing from the homes on the edge of the river to Mill Street, higher up. A boat was kept on Cooper Street for those afraid to cross the bridge. It was operated by a couple of boys who plied up and down the streets, running errands and singing gaily.

All the gates in the fences around the yard were closed to prevent the woodpiles from floating away, and those who had lofts over their kitchens put their poultry there. Yet each year after the water receded, drowned chickens, rabbits, and geese would be found. When the pigeons left their cotes and flew over the inundated streets, the scene suggested the Biblical flood. If the river happened to rise suddenly on washday, the washing remained on the lines stretched from tree to tree, frolicking defiantly above the chaos.

Lacking foundations, houses occasionally floated down the street. One house floated every year while the family remained in it, cooking, sleeping, and observing the annual drama from a first-rate vantage point. While most of the victims were taken into homes on the upper flat no one ever offered to take this family because there were seven children in it.

The Flats children probably got the biggest thrill from the floods. They stayed home from school to help in the emergency and spent their time splashing around, dragging huge cakes of ice and old logs out of the troubled waters.

The village elders, accustomed to the annual excitement, were content to sit on the rickety fences in the sunlight, feet curled above the pickets, puffing at their pipes as they watched the youngsters roping the furniture together, getting it ready to move at a moment's notice.

One of the most eventful floods was that of 1920, when the locks above the Coon Creek dam, fifteen miles upstream, burst. A turbulent flood of water was let loose and that year only five homes on the lower levee remained dry.

In 1928 an embankment was built. When the spring floods of 1929 came, the water began to seep through the embankment and flooded two of the streets. But while the brief rampage had swollen the river higher than in 1920, only six houses stood in water. When the water subsided, the routed residents returned to the dreary scene, scooped out of their kitchens and parlors the wet sand and debris deposited by the Father of Waters, and moved in again.

Folkways

When the immigrants first came to the Flats, they worshiped among the trees along the riverbank or in their homes. The majority of them, being deeply religious, however, soon became troubled by the unorganized state of their spiritual life. Their religious needs came to the attention of the Reverend Friedrich Sieverson, a German Lutheran pastor, who offered them the use of his church "on the hill." Since the pastor could not speak their language the villagers did their best to follow his service in German.

This was an improvement but still an unsatisfactory arrangement. During a church conference at Mankato in 1887 Mr. Sieverson related the plight of the settlers to a colleague, the Reverend Karl Hauser, and asked him to deliver a sermon to the Bohemians, since he was born in Moravia and was familiar with their language. Mr. Hauser complied with the request and was well received by the villagers. As a result, on Thanksgiving Day, 1888, he delivered his farewell sermon to the congregation of the Lanesburg German Lutheran Church, three miles from New Prague, and on the first Sunday of Advent was formally installed in Mr. Sieverson's church as pastor of the Saint Emmanuel Slovak Lutheran Congregation, which had been organized with thirty-six charter members on August 2, 1888. Services were continued there until the villagers obtained their own building, which was located on Cooper Street on the lower flat. Before its purchase by the Slovaks the building had been used as a Sunday school for Swedish children. To buy it the settlers augmented their own slender funds with donations obtained from, to quote Mr. Hauser, "Pillsbury, Lowry, and other friends." A cooper's shop at Washington Avenue on the bluff above the village was converted by Mr. Hauser into a parochial school, and through the influence of a Norwegian Lutheran pastor who was a member of the public school system, school seats were obtained for it. Mr. Hauser served the congregation for five years. He was succeeded by the Reverend D. Z. Lauček, who was followed eleven months later by the Reverend J. S. Mičatek.

During the pastorate of Mr. Mičatek, from 1896 to 1910, the congregation increased until the little church on the Flats became too small to house it. A piece of land was bought at Ontario and Essex streets, in the university section across the river, where a new church was built and dedicated on November 4, 1908. Three years later a parsonage was erected adjacent to the church. When Mr. Mičatek accepted a pastorate at Lansford, Pennsylvania, Mr. Hauser returned to his old charge. Upon Mr. Hauser's retirement in 1920, the Reverend J. Vojtko became pastor. When Mr. Vojtko resigned to join the faculty of Concordia College at Fort Wayne, in 1926, the Reverend J. S. Ontko accepted the pastorate, serving until his death in 1932. He was succeeded by the Reverend J. M. Vrudny. Since 1940 the congregation has been served by the Reverend Ernest J. Reguly.

There were many Roman Catholics among the settlers on the Flats and a considerable number of the Slovaks were Greek Catholics, but neither of these groups established a congregation so exclusively identified with the Bohemian Flats as the Saint Emmanuel Slovak Lutheran Church. Both the Roman Catholics, who according to one estimate made up about a third of the villagers, and the Greek Catholics worshiped at various churches of their faith "on the hill." Many of the Catholic Slovaks traveled to a distant point in Minneapolis, frequently on foot, to be in a congregation of their own nationality. When asked if those trips on Sundays and holy days were not almost too long, a Slovak housewife shook her head. "Not when you were going to church."

Another religious group, the Free Thinkers, also had adherents in the village. Their interests were chiefly intellectual and social and they often furnished the leadership in social activities of the village not identified with the church. Both Catholic and Protestant churchgoers looked upon them with some misgivings. "They call us rationalists now," says one, explaining that "we take a rational view of religion because science has given us a little different view of the world than the Bible does."

As the population of the Flats increased through the years, some of the villagers joined denominations hitherto unknown to them. "When I was a girl in Europe," one woman relates, "there were only Catholics and Lutherans, but now there is everything from Seventh-Day Adventists to Baptists. People just start to go to church. When they find out it isn't Lutheran at all, they stay in it anyway."

A secular organization, the *Sokol*, also played a prominent part in village life. This famous gymnastic society, resembling the German *Turnverein*, was represented in the village by several units at various times. Proficiency in drills, demonstrations, and tournaments of the *Sokols* was a matter of great pride. Fathers and sons often worked together in them. In addition to their athletic programs, the *Sokols* sponsored study classes, as well as dances, picnics, and other community recreations.

Music was in the blood of all these people, and like all folk music it was changed by each one to please his fancy. There was even a variant, sung by the younger people, of the Czech national hymn, "Where Is My Home?" Of this hymn one girl says, "When they pull away from the shores in Europe, they all lean over the railings and sing that song. They open meetings with it and sing it at least once when they have lectures or educational programs. In the homes, though, it is mostly hummed because the words are so sad."

After their peaceful life along the riverbank, when the city officials came to evict the residents of the Flats to make way for municipal improvements, the Czechs among the villagers sang the song with full hearts:

[28

> *Waters thro' its meads are streaming,*
> *Mounts with rustling woods are teeming,*
> *Vales are bright with flowerets rare,*
> *Oh, earth's Eden, thou art fair!*
> > *Thou art my home, my fatherland!*
>
> *By the towers of God, 'tis bounded;*
> *By the noblest sons surrounded;*
> *True and light of heart are they,*
> *Firm and bold in deadly fray,*
> *Offspring grand of dear Bohemia,*
> > *Thou art my home, my fatherland!*

Favorite musical instruments were the accordion, violin, and mouth harp; possibly the bagpipe, too, was heard under the Washington Avenue bridge. This instrument, which differs somewhat from the Scotch pipes, is described by a Czech as having "a little bag with a goat's head on it. They place the bag under their arm and, pressing their arm in and out of the bag, they pump air into it. It makes a sound something like the clarinet or flute." The Czech national dance, resembling a quadrille or an old-time square dance, is composed of twenty-two old folksongs played in succession, the steps changing with the music. It was often performed in the village.

The music of Slovakia sounded through the streets and in the homes of the Flats even more insistently, perhaps, than that brought over from the Bohemian provinces, and Slovak dances were frequent and jolly affairs. Before the Irish drifted away from the village they danced too. With fiddles urging them on, one of their Slovak neighbors remembers, the Irish danced such jigs and reels as were a wonder to watch.

The little wooden church under the bridge was used for rehearsals by the village band, led for a time by Michael Jalma, the conductor of the university band. Others of the music-loving immigrants sang in the village choir. "Down there in the Flats we sang all day long," says one. "But then, why shouldn't we?"

The Slovaks seem to have clung more tenaciously to their old-country customs than did the other Flats groups. By thus preserving so many of their native folkways, the Slovaks contributed even more prominently than the Czechs to the richness of color which characterized everyday life in the community.

Hobbies of earlier days in another land were carried over to these Mississippi flats. Those who had herded goats or cows fashioned flutes from slices of bark. Farmers who in Bohemia had whiled away the winter nights whittling dolls for their daughters, finishing them with gay paint, continued the craft. Baskets were woven from split willow branches. The gourds that during the summer had been encouraged to climb over the riverbanks were now painted for "charm strings," to be sold in the spring to visitors strolling through the village on Sunday afternoons.

The women no longer wove fabrics from the flax they had raised, as in the old country. Instead they sewed dresses for the children from scraps of material on hand and from remnants bought in shops and clothing factories. Many children of the Flats had never worn dresses with both sleeves matching until they began to go to school.

At an early age girls were taught needlework and embroidery. Some bought bright thread from the stores and some spun their own and had it dyed at the textile factories. A gift was almost always something made by hand at home. Slovak girls wore three or four petticoats beneath their skirts, with wide lace trimming at the bottom, knitted by their mothers or older sisters.

Especially picturesque was the Slovak wedding. Language difficulties, which had so hampered pastors in conducting church services in the early days, were likewise an obstacle to the proper performance of the wedding ceremony. German pastors who did not speak Slovak performed the marriage rites for Slovak couples who did not understand German. An elderly resident of the Flats says of her wedding, "I do not know what the minister is saying. My uncle pull my arm and say 'Come, now you been married.'"

Despite this difficulty marriage was the most elaborate of all the holy or festive occasions celebrated by the Slovaks.

Native ideas of dancing, eating, and drinking persisted, and as much as possible of the old ritual of the European wedding was retained. A week or two before the wedding day two or three men from the bridal party made the rounds of the Flats, inviting the villagers to the wedding. As badges of identification the men wore roses pinned to their shirts or carried canes with bright ribbons tied to them. On the day preceding the nuptials the bride's home and its surrounding grounds were decorated and the street was roped off.

Customs of dress and manners varied among the people, since each village in the old country had had its own traditions. The bride's headdress might be a high crown covered with Christmas-tree balls or wreaths of rosemary—traditionally regarded as a symbol of fidelity—that the bridegroom had braided for her the day before. Or she might wear wide bright ribbons that formed the crown of her beaded veil and streamed to the floor. Her vest might be covered with glistening white sea-beads or long streamers of wide ribbons in red, yellow, or green. Style of embroidery and choice of colors varied with each group, but the type of costume remained the same throughout the community. The embroidered skirts were of heavy homespun; the waists had enormous puff sleeves and gathered necklines. Swirling petticoats billowed beneath skirts into which as many as ten yards of material had been gathered. Ordinarily the dress apron was black with festooned borders, but for the wedding day—and only rarely afterwards—the bride wore a white apron. To wear a gay, braid-bedecked jacket and the cherished shawl from her grandmother's trunk was also the bride's privilege for the festive day.

The men laid aside their American work clothes—denim overalls and rough jackets—and put on their native holiday attire. Bright breeches were tucked into shiny boots. White shirts with full sleeves and close-fitting vests of blue or red, carefully embroidered, were worn again with obvious pleasure. Gay plumes waved from high-crowned hats, and sprigs of rosemary were tied to the feathers with colored ribbon.

While the villagers were busy dressing themselves for the

ceremony, the bride was being lectured by an elderly man who acted as her sponsor. The seriousness of marriage was impressed upon the flustered girl in a talk that was usually lengthy and frequently ended with the girl in tears. Recalling many years later the marriages in the Bohemian Flats, an early resident remarked, "Marriage to the Slovak is a very important step. When they said 'Love, honor, and obey, until death do us part,' they meant just what they said. After the ceremony is over, all the people leave the church and only the bride, the oldest bridesmaid, and the minister remain. The three then kneel at the altar, give thanks for having a husband, and ask the Lord's blessing on the marriage. It's a very beautiful way, but they don't do it any more. They do it quick—the American way."

After the wedding ceremony the party went to the home of the bride's mother for the wedding feast that marked the beginning of three days of festivity. Here the party made merry until midnight, and then left for the bridegroom's home to continue the celebration.

When the first feast was over the bride's sponsor, acting as toastmaster, would suggest that the young couple be helped with a collection. The amount given was usually determined by the nearness of the relationship. Thus relatives would usually place a paper bill in the collection, while friends contributed silver coins. A hundred dollars or more was frequently collected in this manner.

Eating was an important feature of the festivities, and the table was constantly burdened with all the native dishes—bowls of sauerkraut, cheese, chickens, roast pig, *koláče*, and beer. Mushroom soup was kept simmering over a slow fire. Wine kegs were broached and great baskets of fruit consumed.

Hope chests for the newlyweds were provided by the bride's parents. The simpler chests were supplied with homespun linen sheets, a few embroidered towels, and a feather tick. More elaborate sets included wardrobes to last both husband and wife for practically a lifetime. As many as twenty-five costumes were sometimes found in the hope chest. The blouses and skirts were so ample that, no matter how buxom a bride might become, they could still be worn. Needle art was taught to the girls before they finished playing with their dolls and they worked on their hope chests for years. Mothers, aunts, and grandmothers would also contribute their needlework. "When the newlyweds moved to the bridegroom's house," an old inhabitant of the Flats recalls, "they took the bride's bedding and hope chest with them in a big wagon while the wedding party followed, playing the accordion and singing through the streets."

It was also the custom for the bride to distribute gifts to the male relatives of the bridegroom, usually shirts she had made herself. To her husband's mother she often gave a shawl or skirt, to which the groom usually added a gift of his own.

As soon as a girl began to think of becoming a bride, she started to sew and knit baby clothes, always white, often for as many as six children. Bonnets, boots, jackets, and large shawls were made and laid away in bundles tied with wide ribbons. When a child was born the parents waited a week and then had it baptized. At the baptismal party the godfather would stand up and propose an offering for the infant. The baby also received presents from the godmother. Six weeks after its birth the mother and godmother took the child to church, where the pastor prayed with them at the altar and they gave thanks for a safe delivery.

There was ceremony of a less joyous kind when a death occurred in the village. The wake began after the body arrived home from the mortuary and continued until the funeral, with relatives and friends staying all night at the home of the deceased.

In the Bohemian Flats as in the old country holidays were closely associated with the church. The Santa Claus myth was not fostered; mothers told their children at Christmas that the Christ child brought the presents. Christmas began on the evening of December 24 and dinner was not served until the stars came out. In many homes a place was set for the family dead because it was felt that they were present on special occasions. Before the dinner was eaten, families partook of holy bread, brought from the church, which they dipped in honey. Some of this bread was also fed to the cows to insure a plentiful supply of milk during the coming year.

Just as the sun was setting and before the church bells rang for the evening service, young girls who wanted to be married began to sweep the kitchen floor. When the first chime of the bell was heard, they would run outside with the sweepings and look about for a man. The name of the first man a girl saw would be the name of the man she would marry. The boys knew the girls would be coming out, so they waited around their doors. "They not only got a kick out of it but often a kiss," laughs a Slovak father. "The best part of the custom was that it really worked!"

After dinner everyone went to the candlelight service at the church. The first Christmas tree on the Flats was set up there and was decorated with tiny candles of twisted wax. An old resident remembers that "we were so afraid the Christmas tree would burn the little church down that we had two men sitting by it all through the service." Carols were sung and the church windows opened wide, so that the light shone on the snow and the songs could be heard far down the street.

Christmas Day was strictly observed. For many years the villagers forbade all work on this day. They could not even sweep the floors. Visiting was postponed until the following day. The only chores permitted were milking and feeding the cows.

Morning services were held at the church. The girls and women did not take seats but stood in front of the altar during the entire service, which frequently lasted two and a half hours. Sometimes a woman fainted before the service was finished, but it was considered disgraceful to sit down. For this occasion older women wore shawls and young married women wore gaily decorated hats, which were later put away until the next Christmas.

The dinner was prepared on the preceding day and typically consisted of mushroom or beef soup, roast pork or fowl, fish and potatoes, sauerkraut, *koláče,* and dried berries or fruits. Sausages were prepared weeks in advance. Heaps of wild nuts, gathered in the fall, were a traditional part of the holiday feast. Christmas bread was made from dried dough cut into small rounds, which were baked and rolled in honey and poppy seed. The old grandmothers told the girls that if they wanted the boys to like them they must put one of the little biscuits under their pillows at night.

The year following the first appearance of the Christmas tree at the church, many homes adopted the custom. In the old country only people of considerable means had had Christmas trees, and some of the villagers had never heard of them until they came to America. The first home Christmas trees in the Flats were decorated by the children with small homemade cookies, nutshells painted in bright colors, bits of rags or paper, and small candles of twisted wax. Long strings of popcorn and cranberries were also used, in the American fashion.

The custom of exchanging gifts during the Christmas season was not general in old Bohemia, but it was universally adopted in the Flats. The women crocheted square shawls, or fascinators, and made bright sweaters and socks. Boys carved wall plaques from blocks of wood salvaged from the Mississippi. Girls fashioned dolls from straw and rags and finished them off with eyes of bright beads. Families exchanged complete dinners, packing them in split-willow baskets and sending them up the road with the children, who stopped at each house along the way to sing Christmas carols and gather cookies or pennies in return. The church choir also made the rounds of the village, singing carols in front of each home.

New Year's Eve, called St. Sylvester's by some of the Flats dwellers, was celebrated in the streets or in the beer house. They played music and danced all night, and welcomed the new year just like their fellow Americans "on the hill." In the early days the lads gathered on the streets, formed circles, and fired guns into the air three times. This custom,

35]

known as "shooting the witches," apparently had no significance when practiced here; its original intent, however, was to frighten away any witches that might be lurking in the neighborhood. The holiday season ended with Epiphany, January 6, which was marked by a church service and was said to be in commemoration of the journey of the three Wise Men to Bethlehem.

St. Valentine's Day, when, so it was believed, the birds began their mating, was observed by the village swains who came bringing large, heart-shaped cookies to their sweethearts early in the evening. These cookies, baked especially for the day, were decorated with designs made of colored sugar or red candy. Paper valentines apparently were not in favor.

The *Morena*, a custom of Slovak origin, was also celebrated annually in the village. When spring was well on its way, the boys made a dummy of straw or hay, usually in the form of a woman, and carried it to the river, singing as they went. There it was thrown into the water as the boys sang "Drown the winter!" The ritual, thought to be of heathen origin, symbolized the banishment of sickness and the diseases of winter and was supposed to bring good crops.

Although the villagers were accustomed to singing at their tasks, grandmothers cautioned the children to "hush the song" when the Lenten season began. One old resident recalls that her grandmother always collected all the piano rolls and victrola records and locked them in her trunk until after Easter. When the children were left alone in the house during this season, one of them would station himself behind the curtains to watch the hilltop while another played the piano or hovered over the victrola. "We always saw them coming back in time and scrambled to get the trunk locked again. We never did get caught."

Easter was celebrated much as in the old country. In most of the Slovak homes a special cheese was made the night before Easter. Eggs, milk, and nutmeg were boiled together and stirred until the mixture was curdled and all the water had cooked off; it was then squeezed through a fine cloth and the strained curds were patted into a flat round and tied off in quarter sections with string. By the next evening the cheese, now pronounced ripe, was a favorite part of the Easter supper.

Another Easter custom was the braiding of willow sticks, three to a bundle; the bundle was then tied every few inches with bits of bright rags. Singers wandered about the village, bundles in hand, singing holy songs in their native tongue and collecting red eggs as prizes.

The first Monday of Easter week was known as "sprinkler day." The boys roamed the streets with toy guns and trick containers filled with water. Any girl they met was likely to be sprinkled. Girls caught at the spring were doused generously and some of the squealing victims were dragged into the river. A girl thus caught was obliged to reward her captor with a bun or an invitation to dinner in gratitude for the luck supposed to be bestowed upon her by the sprinkling. The wetter she became, the better her luck would be. On the following day, however, it was the boys' turn to be wary, for the tables were turned and the girls waited behind sheds and boulders to catch the boys, sprinkle them, and collect the rewards.

On Whitsunday the villagers hung wreaths of basswood and small birch in each room of the house and over the door to celebrate the Ascension. Eight days later the wreaths were taken down and burned. On Whitsunday, too, a youth would slip into his sweetheart's front yard and plant a pair of trees by the gate as a symbol of his love for her.

"Superstitions about the evil eye were not prevalent among them," a Slovak pastor said, "although I do remember one. If they happened to be out calling, or if they were entertaining at home, and they suddenly began to feel drowsy or to have a headache, they believed that an evil eye had been cast upon them. The mother of the home would stand before a wood fire with a pan of water and drop seven pieces of charcoal into the pan, offering a prayer as she did so. The fire was then extinguished and the water given to the patient to wash in. Sometimes three sips of water were taken as a sure cure. I have never tried it," the clergyman continued, "but the woman who told me about it claimed that it really worked." The *palina* plant that hung outside their doors was not there to ward off the evil eye, as strangers sometimes thought, but was only being dried, to be used later for "stom'aches" and to flavor soups.

In the early days of the settlement a doctor was seldom called down to the Flats, the villagers being more disposed to trust their own homemade remedies. If an old woman took off her wedding ring and tied it around the neck of a sick child, she was resorting to an old-time cure for fever. Bread and milk poultices, or bacon, or salt mixed with grass or cabbage leaves were used to heal sores and cuts. If infection set in, it was thought wise to cover the wound with cooked potato. A frequent visitor to the Flats recalls having seen there "a kind of steam bathhouse, quite a big affair, that boiled the germs right out." Homemade cures, of course, were known to be useless in treating ailments commonly recognized as dangerous. Then someone was sent "to the city" to fetch a doctor. Neither for him nor the patient nor the patient's family was it always a happy experience. The story is still told of a doctor who insisted on fresh air for a patient and, meeting opposition from the patient's relatives, determinedly smashed the bedroom window.

For a time Mr. Kokesh, the Flats grocer, had competition from the village midwife, Mrs. Prachticky, who started a grocery store in her front-room window. Her business suffered, however, from inattention. Too many little white or red bonnets, announcing the birth of a boy or girl, contributed to neglect of her other trade. Former residents cannot recall that a child of the Flats ever was born in a hospital. In Slovakia there had been a midwife in every community, provided by the government; the Slovaks in America provided their own. The midwife of the Flats was also the village dressmaker, since for years she owned the only sewing machine in the community.

Although the diverse nationalities that comprised the Bohemian Flats lived in harmony with one another, a mild

[38

form of group rivalry persisted through the years. A little story frequently recounted by the Czechs goes something like this: One Slovak asks another, "What would you do if you were made Emperor?" The other Slovak replies, "If I were made Emperor, I would put fresh straw in my wooden shoes every day." Then the first Slovak says, "Oh! If I were made Emperor, I would make milk to run through the river. Then I would just lie on my stomach and drink it."

Czechs are fond of telling this anecdote because, they say, it shows how impractical the Slovaks are and how much they need the Czechs to mother them.

"We were all nationalities down there," says a Slovak mother who lived on the lower flat before 1900. "It was like a whole world in a little space. Everybody was friendly." Her next-door neighbors, she remembers, were Irish, and when she arrived from the old country she made her first attempts at English conversation with them. Recalling the occasion she laughs and wonders whether, if she had really learned English from them, she might not now be speaking with a rich Kerry brogue.

Farewell, Bohemia!

For many years the settlers of the Flats continued their peaceful existence along the river, undisturbed by the march and clamor of the great city above their heads. Outsiders looked down from the bluff behind the village or from the bridge, watching "those little people" with curiosity or idle familiarity. Visitors wandered through the strange streets, charmed by the quaint, Old World air of the place.

Artists and university students also discovered the pictorial values of the village, though not until some of its older and most authentic color was already gone. Dewey Albinson, a former Twin City artist, pronounced it "the one bit of atmosphere in the whole city of Minneapolis." He spent many days among the villagers and made friends with some of them. Anthony Angarola, another artist, was strongly attracted to the village and felt a certain kinship with it because it reminded him in many ways of his family's native Italian town. Don Methven, Arthur Kerrick, Elmer Young, George Runge, Bob Brown, and other artists made it the subject of their work. S. Chatwood Burton, professor of fine arts at the University of Minnesota, came down to the Flats, rented a squat little cottage with a sky-blue door, and made it over into a studio.

When the artists first appeared the villagers, always apprehensive of possible ridicule, were suspicious of their intentions. Later this feeling of distrust vanished. Sometimes the children were induced to hold a pose long enough to be painted, and many a Flats housewife found herself immortalized on an artist's canvas. In etchings, oil paintings, water colors, and other media the Flats have been portrayed from every angle. The pictures have been exhibited in American cities and, in at least one instance, in Europe. "I saw one of the paintings once," a woman of the lower flat says. "They had me standing on the front porch with a tub of dried leaves. It was very nice."

As the years passed, some of the original settlers left the Flats. A number had saved a little money each week from their earnings and gradually accumulated enough to buy lots "on the hill." Others were induced to move away by their sons and daughters, who wanted running water and bathtubs. Many of the villagers made new friends in the shops and stores in which they worked, acquired new interests and activities, and were slowly drawn out of the village. Their places were always taken by newcomers, however, and life on the Flats went on as before. But catastrophe was approaching.

In 1915 came the first rumbles of the gathering storm. The city of Minneapolis started condemnation proceedings against certain property on the Flats under the general eminent domain law, "with the intention of using same in connection with adjoining lands for wharfage and railroad purposes." The residents of the Flats heard that the city intended to seek out the owners of the riverbank property, purchase the land, and evict the villagers. Some of the Flats dwellers, recalling the prediction of the real-estate agents half a century before as to the future value of the land, believed that the prophecy was now on its way to fulfillment. They expected to sell their land at a good price and move their houses up on the hill, where they could have modern conveniences. Many, however, valued their homes along the river more than modern conveniences and awaited with anxiety whatever action might follow the rumors.

Litigation involving on the one hand the attempts of the property owners to show title to their holdings and on the other the city's condemnation proceedings was begun immediately. Some of the residents thought they had title to the land secured through purchase. Others believed they held title through squatters' rights. Apparently both groups were ignorant of property laws.

The dispute dragged on until 1923, when Mr. C. H. Smith, a real-estate operator, brought action in Hennepin County District Court to dispossess fifteen Flats dwellers for non-payment of rents. They resisted and refused to move. The case was argued in court and by agreement an injunction was granted permitting the residents to retain their homes pending trial of the court actions they had brought to quiet title. They were required to post bonds of two hundred and fifty dollars each to protect Mr. Smith from loss of rents.

Eight of the Flats dwellers, headed by John Medvec, described in the press as a leader in Little Bohemia for many years, brought the actions to quiet title. Other residents contributed loans and gifts of money, since they regarded the suits as test actions, involving them equally with the persons bringing the suits. Fifty contributions were represented in the bonds, totaling $1,750 for seven of the eight families involved in the action. The eighth, a widow, was unable to raise the money. She vacated her home, went to live with a neighbor, and offered the house for sale. There was no buyer.

A touching highlight of the testimony in Mr. Medvec's case, the first to be tried, to prove he had a squatter's right to his cottage, was his statement: "I bought that little house in May 1884. I paid $210 for it but never paid for the land. I'm there all the time. I move in the spring because the river rolls over my floor. I raised my family there." He was then over seventy years old, and his big mustache quivered with agitation as he spoke. He testified that he had never paid any rent except once when his wife was frightened by an attorney representing Mr. Smith and had given him a few dollars. He also testified that he had paid no taxes.

Summoned for the plaintiff, Mr. C. C. Leland testified, in a courtroom crowded with residents of the Flats, that he and his wife, Mary Leland, had been the owners of the land on which the homes of the Flats dwellers stood, that he had purchased it from Dorilus Morrison, a prominent Minneapolis pioneer, and had sold it to Mr. Smith in 1921. Mr. Leland produced an abstract of the deed, which traced the land from the original government grant down to C. C. and W. D. Washburn, to Dorilus Morrison, and then to himself.

On November 14, 1923, District Judge W. C. Leary ruled that the squatters must pay rent or move. This decision was made in Mr. Medvec's case and in that of Mike Sabol, another old-time resident of the Flats. By stipulation the decision was applied to the other five cases. Judge Leary decided that Mr. Smith had shown a clear title to the land and that Mr. Medvec and Mr. Sabol must pay $139 and $110, respectively, in back rent. He gave them thirty days of grace in which to pay or move out.

When the news of the court decision spread through the Flats there was great excitement and bitterness. Groups of women gathered in the back yards and talked it over. "We won't move and we won't pay," they decided. Militantly clutching their broom handles they announced that they would fight all attempts to evict them, while they anxiously waited for their men to return from the mills and factories.

The men were equally resolute. "We built this house and it belongs to us," declared John Medvec. "The land belongs to the river, if anybody. That's the property of the government. We'll pay taxes, but it isn't fair to ask rent for a riverbed."

"We'll pay the city willingly," added Annie Romado, Medvec's neighbor. "They gave us two arc lights and a fire hydrant and schools for our children. But if they [the owners] push their claim for rent, I'll ask damages for the floods that have made us live in the upstairs during the spring and turned the streets into a lake."

"When we have the floods down here and our houses are full of mud and water, Smith stops his big automobile up there on the bridge and looks down at us," complained a woman who had lived on the Flats for seventeen years, "but that's as near as he ever comes to doing anything for us. What right has he to come around now and try to get rent?"

43]

When the period of grace expired and the Flats dwellers had neither moved nor paid the rents, half a dozen policemen attempted to eject fifteen families from their homes. A riot followed in which practically every able-bodied person on the Flats stormed the beleaguered officers of the law with sticks and broom handles. A patrol wagon with a load of reinforcements was rushed to the scene. At about the same time several large moving vans appeared in the Flats, and workmen began to carry furniture out of the houses. Execrations, threats, and orders filled the air, and general havoc prevailed. The situation was getting squally indeed when a lawyer rushed in with an injunction, which he served on the whole ejectment army, and calm was restored.

There was talk of carrying the fight to the Minnesota Supreme Court, but the villagers dropped plans for an appeal and agreed to pay back rent to Mr. Smith and court costs totaling $110 from the bonds posted by the tenants. The third party to the complicated litigation, the city, promptly pressed for a decision in its condemnation suit. By the new year, the fate of almost all the Flats area was no longer in doubt. Nevertheless, many villagers, grimly tenacious, determined to stay until the end. But many more decided not to wait. Moving days were frequent now.

"It appears that life down on the Mississippi river flats nowadays 'ain't so nice like it used to be,' " commented Lorena Hickok, staff writer of the *Minneapolis Tribune*, in March 1924.

"Fat geese and fat children and fat puppies still waddle contentedly about in the rich black March mud. Square-faced Czech mothers, with little white shawls over their heads and exotically dressed infants in their arms, still chatter sociably from fence to fence. And yet—life on the river flats seems to have lost something of its savor.

"Spring is coming to the river flats—spring without a flood. The river is so low now that you can almost wade across. It looks as though it were not more than half as wide as it was a year ago at this time, and even a year ago there was no flood.

"Spring is coming, and soon the bluffs across the river will be soft and feathery and green—'just like in the old country.' But this prospect arouses no gaiety in the hearts of the river flatters.

"Spring is coming with Italian skies and floods of golden sunlight and warm friendly dust to replace the snow and mud. Already two shiny new Fords have found homes on the river flats. And they're tearing down the Northern Pacific railroad bridge that used to frown down upon the little blue and green and salmon houses. That ought to let in a lot more spring sunshine. Everybody ought to be happy, and yet something has gone from the river flats—something including about one fourth of the population.

"All along the narrow cluttered streets of the river flats this spring, you'll see vacant houses. That robin's-egg blue house with the red and yellow window sashes—you can pick it out from the street car window as you cross the Washington Avenue bridge—is empty now. The windows that used to look so gay with their flower plants stare at you lonesomely as you pass. Empty, too, is the snug little brown house with the wide porch and green window sashes, down where the water's edge used to be. So is the gray cabin with the sky-blue door that S. Chatwood Burton, the artist from the university, used to use for his studio. The salmon pink house with the green window sashes is not to get a new coat of paint this year. There's a *For Sale* sign on the quaint dark little grocery store, and a spirit of moving is in the air."

The villagers were, it was true, moving out of their life-long homes on the Flats, but they faced the news reporters, who had come to look over the scene, with stubborn pride.

"Moving out?" asked John Medvec in answer to their queries, with a look of surprise on his face and a lift of his shaggy eyebrows. "Moving out? Where'd you hear anybody was moving out?"

A child, squirming under the strangers' questions, improvised shyly. "Things might fall off the bridge." Annie Rollins' rosy-faced mother shook her head. "No understand English so good" was her amiable comment.

45]

In 1928 the city made a survey of the Flats. Photographs of every house were taken. There were fifty-nine houses and the church still standing—all spotless and neat, "rag rugs on the floors, and featherbeds, every one so high you couldn't see the top of it."

Once more the unyielding survivors of the Flats settlement made up their minds to carry the struggle against "the rich guys" to the courts. Ground rent again became a fighting phrase in legal hearings. On the night of May 31, 1928, Mayor George E. Leach made a sudden and dramatic appearance in the village. "Straw hat on the back of his head, half smoked cigar between his fingers, he talked things over with them, heard their side of the story, made a speech in which he assured them a square deal—and had his picture taken with half of the juvenile population hanging onto his coat-tails."

It was John T. O'Donnell, assistant city attorney, accompanying Mr. Leach, who explained to the villagers the standing of their case in the courts. Following Mr. O'Donnell's talk, the mayor spoke. "I've lived in Minneapolis all my life," he said, "and I can't remember a time when you people were not living down here on the Flats. Perhaps you have no legal rights to this land—the courts must decide that. But in your fight for your homes I sympathize with you. To have his own home—that is a chance that every American citizen should have."

The mayor's speech met with general approval. Children crowded around, dogs got in everybody's way while hunting for their masters, mothers with chubby infants in their arms appeared from all directions, and amid waving flags and banners a hastily printed sign was raised, bearing the slogan "Vote for Mayor George E. Leach." There was much hand-shaking; newspaper cameras clicked; and when the mayor's long gray touring car ascended the hill it was agreed up and down the Flats that it had been a very large evening indeed.

But despite the good feeling engendered by the mayor's visit the villagers were soon to realize the hopelessness of their fight against encroaching industry. In the spring of

1929 the city prepared to increase its barge terminal facilities on the Flats. River traffic had been resumed in 1926 when the S. S. *Thorpe* came up from St. Louis.

In June the city officially notified fifty-two claimants that it was about to resume condemnation proceedings. The following month an appraisal committee began an evaluation of the property and was courteously treated by the villagers. At this time the village had only about one hundred inhabitants, all that remained of the five hundred or more who had lived there a few years before.

The city's condemnation proceedings were not contested by the villagers. Values averaging about a thousand dollars each were placed upon the one- and two-room houses of the Flats dwellers, and approximately thirty-two thousand dollars was offered for the ten acres or so of property needed for the coal terminal. The announcement of the awards produced so many "owners" that, as a writer for the *Minneapolis Journal* wrote, "they will soon have to wear badges to keep from selling to each other."

Although a few villagers protested against the coming eviction and some bitterly lamented the necessity that forced them to give up their homes, the majority were resigned to their fate. In February 1931 fifty eviction notices, effective April 1, were issued by the city. The removal was ordered so that workmen could begin cleaning up the area before the construction of the new coal docks and the dredging of the river.

March found the villagers demolishing their homes. They stacked the lumber in piles and then hauled it to their new places of residence "on the hill." By April 1 all who had received the notice to vacate had disappeared—all except Frank Badnarek and his dog.

For many weeks, while houses were falling around him, Frank merely sat and watched. He had lived on the Flats for forty-two years and now, though all his friends were leaving, he was determined to remain, he and his dog. When the trucks came and dumped gravel all around him, he watched —and held his ground. He hoisted a flag over the roof of his

47]

little shack and watched the proceedings. He didn't mind a few inconveniences as long as he could get in and out of his home. But when one of the trucks backed up to his front door and left a load of gravel on his doorstep, Frank capitulated. The flag that had waved defiantly in the breeze was hauled down; he removed his belongings and tore down the shack, the only home he had known for many years. Sitting on his trunk, flanked by a bushel basket and a washtub packed with odds and ends collected in the course of a lifetime, he wondered where he would go. He had been injured in an accident some years back and was unable to work.

"What can a man do with all those trucks?" he said to newspaper reporters who came to see the last lone defender of the Flats.

From
the Flats Kitchens

Potato and Watercress Soup

Beef stock
6 or 8 potatoes
1 large bunch watercress
8 egg yolks

1 pint milk
1/2 cup grated cheese
Salt and pepper
2 tablespoons butter

Grate raw potatoes, put them in the boiling stock, and simmer for about 30 minutes. Mash the cooked potatoes or rub them through a sieve. A few minutes before serving, add the watercress, finely chopped. Have egg yolks ready in a soup tureen, mixed well with a pint of warm milk and the 2 tablespoons butter. Pour soup into the tureen over the egg mixture. Season with salt, pepper, and cheese.

Fish Soup

1 1/2 cups fish stock
1/2 can pea soup
1 cup vegetable stock
Salt and peppercorns
Fish roe

A few tablespoons soured
  cream
Thin slices lemon peel
1 tablespoon vinegar
Cooked fish

Mix strained fish stock, vegetable stock, and pea soup. Stir well. Season with salt and peppercorns, and cook slowly for 15 minutes. Add a few pieces of cooked fish, also fish roe and vinegar. Pour into a soup tureen, adding soured cream and lemon peel. Serve with chunks of fried bread.

Sour Mushroom Soup

1 pound chopped dried
  mushrooms
1 small onion

2 quarts sauerkraut
  juice
1 tablespoon flour

Soak mushrooms in warm water, then drain. Boil in the sauerkraut juice until tender, about 1 hour. Cut up the onion and fry in butter until brown. Add flour and brown. Then add mushrooms and kraut juice; simmer.

Sauerkraut Roll

1 1/2 pounds ground pork	2 cups partly cooked rice
1 cabbage	Sauerkraut juice
	Salt and pepper to taste

Mix pork, rice, and seasoning. Pick off the outer whole leaves of the cabbage and place them in boiling water to soften. Then remove leaves from water and fill with pork mixture. Roll the filled leaves and pin with toothpicks. Place rolls in sauerkraut juice and boil about 2 hours. Rolls may be baked instead of boiled by putting them in a baking pan, adding water, and baking until tender.

Potato Rolls

Select large potatoes, long and well shaped. Make two or three holes in each, lengthwise, with apple corer. Fill holes with rolls of bacon, Vienna sausage, little pig sausage, or cheese. Bake until tender.

Potato Dreams

1 cup mashed potatoes, seasoned	1 teaspoon salt
1/2 cup flour	1/4 cup milk
1/2 teaspoon baking powder	1/2 cup grated cheese
	1 beaten egg

Mix ingredients and roll dough as for biscuits. Cut out with doughnut cutter; fry in deep fat.

Potato Gravy

1 onion	1 cup riced potatoes
Flour	Mixed spices
2 cups water	Salt and pepper to taste

Fry onion in a small portion of grease. Add flour and brown. Add water, mixed spices, salt, pepper, and riced potatoes. Boil slowly. Strain and serve.

Potato Dumpling

2 cups raw grated potatoes	4 slices stale white bread, soaked and wrung dry
1/2 cup flour	
1 teaspoon salt	1 egg

Mix ingredients and roll out dough in pieces about 3 inches long and 1/2 inch thick. Drop into boiling water and boil 15 minutes.

Another kind of dumpling may be made from the same recipe, except that less flour is added and the dough is consequently somewhat thinner. Dip dough from mixing bowl with a spoon and drop into boiling water. Boil 10 minutes and serve with fried cabbage.

Perchy

2 cups flour   1 egg
1 teaspoon salt   5 tablespoons water
1/4 pound butter

Mix salt, egg, and water. Add the flour to make a soft dough. Roll out thin and cut into 2 1/2-inch squares. Place on the square a spoonful of poppy-seed filling or any cooked fruit filling, pinch into a triangle, and drop into boiling water. Cook about 10 minutes. When done, the triangles will come to the top of the water. Remove triangles from water and lay on board. Sprinkle with cold water. Brown 1/4 pound of butter and pour over *perchy*.

Lokše

2 cups cold boiled   1 cup flour
potatoes, riced   Pinch of salt
Melted butter

Mix ingredients, roll thin, cut in pieces like pancakes, bake light brown; or bake in a large, thin, flat cake and cut into wedges. After removing from oven or griddle, cover with a towel for 15 minutes to soften. Spread with melted butter, using pastry brush or feather brush. Roll these pancakes or wedges into cylinders and place in pan or casserole close together to prevent unrolling. Reheat and serve warm. (More potatoes and less flour may be used.)

Koláče

1 cake compressed yeast   1/2 cup melted butter
1 cup warm water   2 beaten eggs
1 teaspoon sugar   10 cups flour

Scald milk, add sugar and salt, and let cool to lukewarm. Then add mixture of yeast and warm water. With this blend half the flour and beat until smooth. Add beaten eggs, melted shortening, then the rest of the flour.

Let stand to rise in a warm place. Knead dough and let rise again for about 1 hour. Roll out dough to thickness of about half an inch. Cut into 2 1/2-inch squares and fill.

Suggested fillings: 1/2 pound very dry cottage cheese (smooth with fork, add beaten egg, pinch of salt, and 2 tablespoons sugar); cooked prunes, apricots, or other fruit (stone the stewed fruit, mash with fork, and sweeten); poppy seed (grind 1 cup poppy seed and add 1 tablespoon honey, 1/2 cup sugar, and 1/2 cup hot water; or soak 1 cup poppy seed in 1 cup milk, let stand for several hours or in refrigerator overnight, make a custard pudding mixture, add the soft poppy seed and honey, cook over slow fire about 15 or 20 minutes, then let cool).

Place heaping teaspoonful of filling on each square, pinch the four corners firmly together, let rise again for about 1 hour. Bake 45 minutes in moderate oven, or until golden brown.

Index

53]